GOOD DEEDS, GOOD DESIGN

GOOD DEEDS, GOOD DESIGN: COMMUNITY SERVICE THROUGH ARCHITECTURE
EDITED BY BRYAN BELL

PRINCETON ARCHITECTURAL PRESS, NEW YORK

Published by
Princeton Architectural Press
37 East Seventh Street
New York, New York 10003

For a free catalog of books, call 1 800 722 6657.
Visit our web site at www.papress.com.

Cover: David Harp © 2001
Frontispiece: Daniel Lama

This publication is supported by grants from the National Endowment
for the Arts, the Richard H. Driehaus Foundation, the Graham
Foundation for the Advancement of Fine Arts, and the American
Institute of Architects College of Fellows.

NATIONAL
ENDOWMENT
FOR THE ARTS

Editing: Clare Jacobson
Editorial assistance: Nicola Bednarek and Linda Lee
Design: Omnivore, Alice Chung and Karen Hsu

Princeton Architectural Press would like to thank: Nettie Aljian,
Janet Behning, Megan Carey, Penny (Yuen Pik) Chu, Russell Fernandez,
Jan Haux, Krystina Kaza, Mark Lamster, Nancy Eklund Later, Nancy
Levinson, Katharine Myers, Jane Sheinman, Scott Tennent, Jennifer
Thompson, Joe Weston, and Deb Wood —Kevin C. Lippert, publisher

Library of Congress Cataloging-in-Publication Data
Good deeds, good design : community service through architecture /
Bryan Bell, editor.— 1st ed.
     p. cm.
Includes bibliographical references.
 ISBN 1-56898-391-3 (alk. paper)
 1. Low income housing—United States 2. Architects and community—
United States. 3. Architectural services marketing—United States.
I. Bell, Bryan, 1959–
 NA7540.G66 2003
 728'.086'24—dc21

                              2003013288

ACKNOWLEDGMENTS

First I would like to thank each of the authors of this publication, not only for their essay but for the work that it represents. Thanks to Design Corps' Board and Fellows, especially to the assistant editors: Kindra Welch, Andrea Dietz, Victoria Ballard Bell, Stacy Safko, and the Structures for Inclusion conference chairs: Melissa Tello, Kathy Koehler, Jeff Evans, and Will Hartzog. Great thanks also to Clare Jacobson, my editor at Princeton Architectural Press, who has been a tremendous help on this project from the very beginning. And my deepest thanks and love to my wife, Victoria, and to my parents, Rubie and Bryan, for their unending support.

DESIGNING FOR THE 98% WITHOUT ARCHITECTS

BRYAN BELL

BRYAN BELL is the director of Design Corps, a nonprofit architecture firm based in Raleigh, North Carolina, that he founded in 1991. He has taught community design-build at three architecture schools, including twelve projects at the Auburn Rural Studio. In 1995, Bell started the Design Corps Fellowship program, which allows recent graduates to design for the underserved.

People should be able to participate in decisions that shape their lives. And the design of the built environment is one of these decisions. As the technical nature of the built world requires the expertise of architects and planners, it is they who must help people to be involved in these decisions. Architects' greatest contributions can be as the form-givers for others, shaping lives in the most fundamental and personal ways.

Yet only the very few have been able to work with the designers of the built world. In 1995 I saw an article in the *Philadelphia Inquirer* stating that only 2% of new homebuyers worked directly with an architect. Here was the documentation of a feeling I had had since I left working in the architectural office of Steven Holl, where we were serving only the very few, and the benefits of design were out of reach for most.

But how can architects increase the number of people that they serve? First, they must reassess the service and benefits architecture provides. Defining those is necessary, because the greater public—the 98% without access to architects—certainly does not understand what architects do, and it is the architect's task, not the public's, to present the reasons that design can help.

Many designers, ranging from people working for large institutions to individuals working on their own, are taking initiatives locally to address the underserved. *Good Deeds, Good Design* advances the best new thoughts and practices in this emerging sector that serves a broader population. The goal of this publication is to help increase the number of people who can benefit from access to design through a new notion of architectural services. Each essay herein raises specific design and social issues, while case studies illustrate both successes and failures.

The essays are the results of a series of conferences called "Structures for Inclusion" that presented the work of for-profit and nonprofit architecture firms, community design centers, and nonprofit organizations. There is some emphasis on single-family housing herein, as that building type allows for a direct working relationship between a few specific individuals and a designer. But other examples, such as public buildings and outdoor spaces, illustrate other benefits of design.

The title *Good Deeds, Good Design* means that projects have been selected that give an equal priority to both. "Good deeds" does not mean, however, that design is a patronizing gift from architects to communities. In all the projects presented here, there is a mutual exchange between the designer and the client, and, in the best cases, a mutual benefit for both. Through a participatory process, these benefits are defined, clearly understood by all, and mutually sought.

Good Deeds, Good Design demonstrates a broad set of approaches to community-based design. By providing evidence and pathways, these show the clear development of an alternative practice of architecture. It is in the spirit of fostering this development and the sharing of linked ideas that these essays are presented here. The best hope for the future is not that these case studies will be repeated, but that they will assist others in moving forward the goal of providing quality design for those currently underserved.

TWO QUESTIONS FOR ARCHITECTURE
ROBERT GUTMAN

ROBERT GUTMAN is lecturer in architecture at Princeton University and Professor Emeritus of sociology at Rutgers University. He is the author of *The Design of American Housing* and *Architectural Practice: A Critical View.*

Two questions are of central concern in this book: What can the architectural community do to increase the supply of housing for low-income groups? How can architects enlarge their contribution to housing design and production?

HOUSING FOR LOW-INCOME GROUPS

Take the first question. To me, the answer is fairly clear. Architects must adopt an advocacy role—they must step outside their usual activity as architects to engage in political action that will encourage the expansion of government programs that underwrite low-income housing construction. Government programs, even in this period when most lower-income housing production is sponsored by nonprofits, remain the predominant basic source of funding.

To some architects, political engagement is regarded as a normal fraction of their professional activity. To others, it is a deformation of their role as architects. Thirty to forty years ago, architects were more inclined to believe that political advocacy was essential to the practice of architecture. Indeed, some architects went so far as to assert that design, when properly deployed, could foster the users' awareness and involvement in politics. Many architects were in the forefront of the assaults on the establishment that were commonplace during the Vietnam War. At Princeton, for example, the architecture school served as the communication center for campus activity after the Kent State killings; and the students in Avery Hall, the architecture school building at Columbia, were central figures in the uprising there. In Paris in 1968, the Ecole students constituted one of the European centers of radical activity.

The enthusiasm for political activity soon paled among architects. It was too strenuous; it demanded too much in the way of sustained organization. It was easy to agree with Michel Foucault that all institutions were by their very nature repressive—it was another matter to imagine and maintain political action or social programs to right the condition.

Those architects who manifested their social consciousness through adoption of a behavioral science model for architectural design became disillusioned in other ways. They discovered that a simple functionalist model of design did not fulfill its ambitions, that buildings and people were too complex to allow a predictable relationship between the organization of space and the organization of people's lives.

I believe this book is one of many signs that the rejection of the political and social dimensions by mainstream architecture over the past thirty years, the substitution of critique for advocacy, leaves out too much of the architectural endeavor. Humanism, Renaissance humanism, which has so often been the source of many ideas of Western architecture after modernism, cannot replace humanitarianism. It is an illusion to argue that architecture is an autonomous discipline. Although the intention behind the spread of this doctrine was laudable —indeed one could argue, given the situation in American architecture, it was necessary and generated a period of enormous formal and intellectual creativity—the idea of autonomy unfortunately was interpreted to mean that architecture could ignore its social context, that it did not have to respond consciously and actively to the political and economic conditions that supported its expression.

I am aware that some participants in the current revival of political interest among architects are worried that to recall the rise, then fall, of an earlier stage of advocacy architecture will undermine the determination of a new generation to invest in the program implied by this book. I actually think it may have the opposite result. Young people who are innovative and radical often are bolstered by an awareness that they are part of a noble historical tradition, that others before them have fought the same battles, perhaps even for similar reasons. It is an advantage for movements, architectural or otherwise, to stand on the shoulders of ancestors.

ENLARGING ARCHITECTS' CONTRIBUTION TO THE HOUSING MARKET

The second question that runs through these essays is how architects can enlarge their contribution to housing design and production. This question is more difficult. Merchant builders, who produce housing for the mass market, control the present system of housing design and production in this country. The system operates by putting the architectural intelligence in a subservient role. The merchant builders and their market researchers invent the ideas that dominate production. This does not mean necessarily that the large merchant builders do not employ architects—they do, hundreds of them— but they use them as scribes, stenographers who translate the harsh speech of the developer into the language of design. Architects in these corporations are never the major decision-makers.

Perhaps the most instructive fact about the American housing production system is that the best opportunities for architects to influence housing design arises in the low-income and affordable-housing sectors, when the housing is owned either by government agencies or by nonprofit organizations, often CDCs, or Community Development Corporations.

Isn't this a curious situation? The two groups that benefit most from the inputs of architects are the social classes at the two ends of the class system: the rich who hire architects to design their often lavish single-family mansions and the lower social groups who generally live in multiple dwellings. Just think of such examples as Robert Venturi and Denise Scott Brown's Guild House, or Charles Moore's South Street project in New Haven, or Frank Gehry's social housing project in Berlin. The mass of the population, the great American middle class, must make do with housing designed by merchant builders.

Since the middle of the nineteenth century, there has been a plethora of initiatives in the United States to bring architectural services to the middle-class home buyer. It was one of the first goals announced in the platform of the American Institute of Architects soon after the founding of the organization in 1857. Seventy years ago, during the Great Depression, the AIA through its Small Homes Bureau began a concentrated effort to make house plans designed by architects available for low fees to ordinary consumers. More recently, architects specializing in residential design have attempted other programs, including writing books that explain how to plan a house and when to call upon the services of an architect. One after another, these programs have largely been abandoned, because the audience was never large enough to make a difference in the business of small offices. All the while, however, from the 1870s to today, architects have remained much involved in the provision of philanthropic housing, the design of housing for the military establishment, housing for workers in war factories, public housing, and affordable housing.

DESIGNING FOR LOW-INCOME HOUSING

Why should architects have greater influence in the design of housing for the lower levels of the class system? I can think of four reasons. First, most of the officials who run the agencies do not have the know-how about housing production to match the skill and experience of the merchant builder. They have no alternative but to seek the assistance of experts.

Second, merchant builders spend the majority of their effort producing single-family housing, either detached or in row form. The design problem in this situation is relatively simple and, once solved, can be repeated over and over. Most low-income housing involves the design of multiple dwellings, which raises numerous issues that are more complex from both architectural and planning perspectives. Greater expertise, such as that possessed by architects, is required to deal with them.

Third, the design of multiple-dwelling *affordable* housing is more complicated than other multiple-dwelling types, largely because of the special demands put on it by public authorities, neighbors, and community sentiment. For example, housing for lower-income groups is often located on sites that are smaller, of peculiar shape, and ridden by pollution and brownfield problems. Design elements must be introduced to hide the projects, adapt to zoning restrictions, and make them appear consistent with surrounding dwellings. The resolution of these issues adds to the expense of the housing and requires great ingenuity and resourcefulness, skills that trained architects are likely to possess.

Finally, nonprofits believe they stand a better chance of obtaining local planning and zoning approvals if they have an architect appear with them at hearings. Remember that the public views architects as the most honest, objective, and responsible actors in the housing-production process. We know this from the many studies that have been conducted in the United States over the past fifty years, in which architects are consistently ranked at the top of occupational prestige scales. Their high status is consistent with the fact that architects are among the very few licensed professionals in the housing-production process.

The low-income and affordable-housing markets are such large markets, and the position of architects is so much more central than in the market for middle-class housing, that it may make sense to concentrate our efforts in catering to this population, especially because there is a tremendous volume of work still to be done here. No more than 5% of the new housing units produced in recent years are affordable. We still are tearing down more low-income units annually than we replace with the HOPE VI and HOME programs. (The HOPE VI program—Housing Opportunities for People Elsewhere—has been a federal program that rehabilitates or rebuilds distressed public housing projects; the HOME program supports the construction and acquisition by local agencies of affordable housing that is sold or rented to lower-income groups.) Affordable units in the United States dropped by 372,000 from 1991 to 1997. The Department of Housing and Urban Development estimates that we are short six million—I repeat, six million—affordable housing units. Here, it seems to me, is where we should be intensifying the application of our energies.

ADDRESSING THE MASS PRIVATE-HOUSING MARKET
To say it makes sense to concentrate in the area of what European architects still refer to as "social housing" does not imply that we should ignore opportunities to influence the mass private-housing market. As difficult as it has been, and continues to be, for the profession to penetrate this market in a significant way, there are some signs that the tradition of housing practice that has dominated in this country may be beginning to change. I am encouraged, for example, by the experience of the New Urbanists. In the debate within the architectural community about the wisdom of New Urbanist proposals, the most important fact about their ideas is often overlooked—namely, that they are the first architectural movement in many decades to whose ideas the public has paid some attention. Their proposals have been adopted by a remarkably wide spectrum of clients, ranging from developers in the

upper middle-class market to the administrators of the HOPE VI program. This is no small achievement, despite the reservations many architects and critics may have about the adequacy of some of their ideas. Their tremendous success portends a very important fact about the architectural scene—namely, that local, regional, and state planning standards *are* being elevated. When this happens, it is an indication that the contribution of architects can play a more important role as advisers to agencies and merchant builders, as propagandists of new ideas, and as actors in the political process.

But to make this really happen, I still believe, requires that we broaden the scope of architecture to incorporate a greater emphasis on social action. Architects must become advocates, even if only advocates for their own competence and their own ideas. In this situation, it may be a good idea to borrow a theme popularized by the feminist movement. No private domain of a person's life, the feminists have argued, is without a political aspect, and there is no political issue that is not ultimately personal. Architecture is, for most of us, our personal life. Because it is, we should realize that architecture always and necessarily has political implications. One method to manifest its political content is to advocate the approach to housing that this book exemplifies.

1 / TOOLS FOR CHANGE

FINDING CLIENTS
BRYAN BELL

Traditionally, architects and clients start their working relationship when the clients, who understand what architecture is and what they need from it, contact the architect. But when architecture is a community service, it is the architect who seeks out the clients.

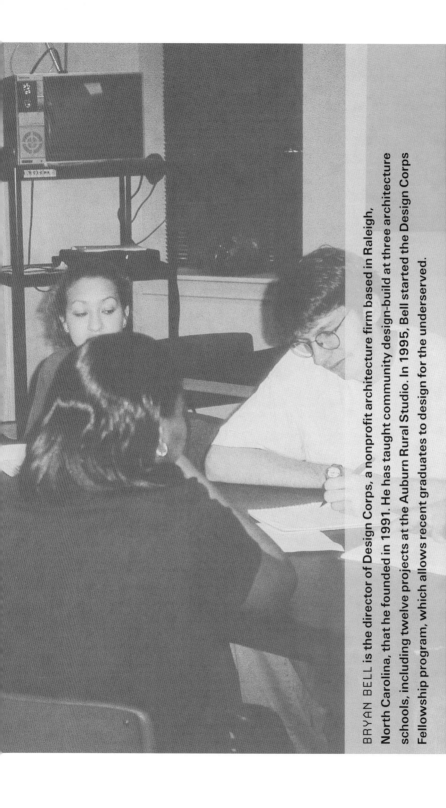

BRYAN BELL is the director of Design Corps, a nonprofit architecture firm based in Raleigh, North Carolina, that he founded in 1991. He has taught community design-build at three architecture schools, including twelve projects at the Auburn Rural Studio. In 1995, Bell started the Design Corps Fellowship program, which allows recent graduates to design for the underserved.

The following are examples of finding clients that give a variety of approaches in making connections between those who need design services and those who can provide design. These are presented not as ideal, but so that others can learn from and improve on these past efforts.

THE PERSONAL APPROACH

As the first house of the Rural Studio, Auburn University's design-build program, neared completion, director Samuel "Sambo" Mockbee started looking for the next family for whom his students could design and build a house. As Mockbee told the story, "I approached a house that appeared to be in bad shape and knocked on the door. Anderson Harris answered the knock, and I asked him if he wanted us to build him a new house. He said, 'Not today, thank you.' That made me feel like a door-to-door salesman."

As we as architects assess the value of our services to the greater public, this story has a cautionary note. Are we, in fact, like door-to-door salesmen whom nobody wants to see, selling something that very few want? The general public, the 98% without access to architects, often do not understand what we do and what we can do for them. As Mockbee used to say, "Architecture has been put on the top shelf, out of the reach of most."

But Mockbee pressed on, and Harris and his wife now live in the second Rural Studio effort, called the "Butterfly House." Furthermore, Harris is now an advocate of design (even though he complains that "the rain blows into the porch sometimes"). It is hard to imagine he ever was not; as visitors tentatively approach his house, Harris's deep voice booms out from the shadows of the inner porch—"keep on coming, keep on coming"—welcoming them to come see the results. Harris now seems as much a part of the Rural Studio as any professor or student, and an ongoing relationship between his family and the program continues.

Designers who are not involved in working for the lower-income sector occasionally criticize the work of the Rural Studio as patronizing and insensitive. This is an important criticism to consider, as designers in any situation can hold power and dominate the decision-making process. Nothing could prove further from the truth in this case, however, as the mutual respect, mutual benefit, and long-term relationships between the Rural Studio and the Harrises are deeper than those between most architects and their clients. In fact, the many architects serving the top 2% could learn a good deal from the respect involved in the Rural Studio's design process.

ESTABLISHING CRITERIA FOR PARTICIPATION

After the Harris house was built, the Rural Studio established a different process for creating partnerships with families. The Hale County Department of Human Resources (DHR), a state-funded social service agency, helped make the best connections between families in need of a house and the design-build program. DHR is typical of community-based agencies that exist in every U.S. county in having intimate grassroots knowledge of issues and individuals in need. In its role as a matchmaker, DHR recommends several families in need for participation in the Rural Studio program. Following these recommendations, "get-to-know-you" meetings take place, and if the chemistry is right, the students and client proceed to creating a project.

In 1999, instructor Stephen Hoffman and I defined criteria to match the goals of the program with a family's situation and their needs based on past lessons. We first asked Rural

Studio students to develop a list that would help us find the best partner in the new house design-build project—to assure that our services would be of use to the family and that they understood what the program involved. A mutual assessment between students and families would take place during two meetings with all family prospects. In the first meeting the family would present their current housing situation and their needs. This was followed by an inspection of their home to assess the physical needs of safety, based on the Department of Housing and Urban Development (HUD) Minimum Property Standards. The second meeting was described as "seeking the poetry," and the students were asked to try to understand what impact a new house could have on the family's problems. The issue of design as a solution to specific needs was to be clarified as much as possible.

Rural Studio students undertook a three-step process to select one family for their design-build program.

For the Rural Studio's fifth project, DHR recommended seven families whom they had informed about the program and the selection process, and who had expressed an interest in participating. The students went through the first meeting with all seven of these families. Based on these interviews, they voted to interview four families in the next step. Finally, two families were selected. A difficult choice then had to be made between greatest need and greatest benefit. While one family had the worst housing conditions, a new house would not address their greatest needs and might reinforce the main problem, which was a physically abusive boyfriend—a new house might encourage him to stay with the family. The second family, a single mother enrolled in a welfare-to-work program, was on a clear path to improving conditions. She felt that their current housing, which was in a HUD rental project, was a threat to the health and safety of herself and her children. In the end, the students unanimously decided to work with the second family, but the complexity of social issues and the limits of design to solve them provided a humbling learning experience for us all.

RESEARCHING ALTERNATIVE CLIENTS

Another approach to finding a client is to undertake research into a specific community or issue, which can reveal social problems in need of a built solution. This was the task at hand during the inaugural session of the Outreach Studio, an extension of the Rural Studio to Auburn students outside of the architecture program. The challenge given to the students at the beginning of the ten-week summer program was to find a project that would meet a community need in Mason's Bend, a small community where the Rural Studio had built many projects.

The students decided to do something that had not been done before: knock on the door of every household in Mason's Bend, beginning a discussion with the community by listening to its members. They mapped every house and resident of the town, a community of 23 houses and 112 people. Mason's Bend consists of three core families: the Bryants, the Harrises, and the Fields. The first two had been recipients of multiple design-build projects by the Rural Studio students. There was the perception of a growing resentment by the Fields because they had not been involved. In fact, a land ownership challenge by the Fields against the Bryants had threatened one of the past projects. The Outreach Studio team decided that their goal would be to work with the Fields to alleviate this rising problem. But communication was difficult in this situation, and the door-to-door efforts were

TOP LEFT: Rural Studio students tell Shannon Sanders-Dudley that they want to work on a new house for her family. TOP RIGHT: The Sanders-Dudley family visited the Rural Studio's dormitory for a day of fun before the design process started. ABOVE: A "slippy slide," made from a garden hose, dishwashing liquid, and salvaged plastic sheets, was the culmination of the family's visit.

not productive. Members of the Field family were skeptical and distrustful, sometimes even hostile of the students' attempts to talk with them.

Finally, Heath Lee Van Fleet, an engineering student, made a breakthrough with the family through an indirect route. He knocked on their door and explained the Outreach Studio's design-build intentions and *its* needs for a project. One of Mary Field's daughters responded that what Van Fleet could do to help was cut the weeds in the back yard. He obliged, realizing he had been misunderstood. Soon after he started, Field's son-in-law Tyrone joined him. Together they cleared the yard and became friends. This became the beginning of the Outreach Studio's conversations with the Fields. It was critical to do something for them to establish some trust. Only then could the students explain the goals of a design-build project and see if this was of benefit to the extended family. Although the students thought they were offering something to the Fields, it was important to be honest and realize that the design-build project was motivated by their own goals as well. It was when they set aside their own agenda to let a relationship form that they made progress.

Subsequent conversations with the Fields helped the Outreach Studio understand a community need in having something for the local children to do. One favorite activity, basketball, occurred in the dirt streets. While the packed red earth was surprisingly effective for dribbling, the game was less than safe and constantly interrupted by traffic. The students proposed a small sitting area and a large basketball half-court and goal. This was completed and meets its purpose as a safe recreation area for the local children. It provides the second "public" space in the community, an active space for the young to complement the more passive area of the adjacent community chapel, which was completed the previous spring by four Rural Studio thesis students.

SURVEYING NEEDS

Other efforts to provide design to the underserved show a similar need for architects to take the first step. At Design Corps, a nonprofit design firm providing architecture services to low-income people, we attempt to serve migrant farm workers by building them well-designed housing. We use a participatory approach to design that requires making meaningful contact with the workers. Our first method of understanding our clients' needs, wants, and localized conditions is to undertake surveys. While we may feel this is of benefit to the workers, it is first of benefit to ourselves in meeting our goals.

Migrant housing design session with mushroom workers and Design Corps fellow Kindra Welch.

Over time we learned how to gather this information more sensitively. We first tried to take these surveys at the workers' homes. This proved to be an unfortunate mistake on our part, as workers often could not communicate openly out of fear of losing their jobs by criticizing their employer's housing. At the same time, they had little opportunity to avoid us and were confused about why we were asking so many questions, despite our efforts to explain. Furthermore, we were possibly interfering with their few minutes of free time or preventing the rest they needed.

We then decided to meet our clients on more neutral ground, at the Migrant Health Care clinics. There, we reasoned, was a place where they were waiting and not busy doing anything else. But Design Corps Fellow Kersten Harries suggested that this would be an intrusion into the workers' private time and would leave them with little choice if we

Sunday mornings at the local flea market were the best time and place for migrant design surveys.

approached them. She moved the surveying effort to Sunday mornings, the real "free time" in a migrant worker's schedule, and met them at flea markets, where they could choose to participate or not. Also, she decided to offer the workers something for helping us. Her first effort was to offer a raffle ticket to win a radio to anyone who completed a survey. However, after one week with this idea, she realized that many of the workers did not have a phone number or even a mailing address to be notified if they won. She found a better approach and offered a cold bottle of water in exchange for a completed survey.

While this example does not show how to find a specific client, it does illustrate how to learn from a community, which can lead to identifying its needs, which can then lead to clients and projects.

As we move to actually designing with a specific client, we strive to meet two guiding principles: disclosing the process and sharing the decision-making. Explaining the design process to the client from the beginning and detailing opportunities for their input help foster a productive working relationship. While designers may be familiar with the design process, too often clients are expected to start a design process on blind faith. Sometimes this faith is rewarded, and other times this faith is betrayed by the designer, even if unintentionally, because the client was unaware of the route and therefore of the destination. Design requires enough faith—because the end product is initially unknown—without increasing client anxiety and confusion through an unclear process.

The other critical element of a productive relationship is a shared decision-making process. Including diverse perspectives in the design decisions adds both practical results and a fresh source of design inspiration. The client is an expert at their use of space and their priorities in terms of allocation of resources. The architect is the expert at translating these into graphic and formal spaces and in the use of materials. This does not suggest that the architect becomes the draftsperson for the client. The architect is the form-giver, but the content for the form comes from the client.

By comparing methods for finding and working with clients from the underserved 98%, architects can begin to establish the best future practices. Communication about methods, such as those documented here, will assure that designers in this emerging area can learn from one another and need not reinvent the wheel by trial and error, making the same mistakes and even harmful missteps. This shared knowledge can begin to make protocols for a practice of design that is truly community based. It will allow the individuals being served to understand the process and to participate in the decisions.

RECONFIGURABLE SYSTEMS
GEORGE ELVIN

For the low-income sector, budgets limit choices to the most common materials and building systems, often resulting in generic designs. But can expression be achieved on a tight budget through flexible systems allowing for customization and changes over time?

GEORGE ELVIN teaches at the University of Illinois at Urbana-Champaign School of Architecture. He has been an associate with firms working on large international projects in Germany and Japan and for ten years ran his own design-build firm in Washington, D.C.

Architects add value to their clients' lives by customizing the fit between their needs and the environment. But what are the options for the 98% of homebuyers who cannot afford the services of an architect? Can we envision new tools and methods that empower them to shape their own environments to their needs? One emerging technology that may help accomplish this goal is that of reconfigurable construction systems—changeable assemblies of building components like walls, ceilings, and floors. These systems can make it possible to modify a building during and after construction at little or no cost to the user. They allow building users to personalize their environments and allow architects in service to the community to increase user input to the design process and reduce the time they spend redrawing changes. The increased adaptability of buildings using reconfigurable construction systems can conserve environmental resources, save money, and preserve our architectural heritage by encouraging reuse and redesign of existing structures. While no current construction system attains the ideal of total reconfigurability, four current approaches to this problem begin to address the issues: remodeling, custom systems, off-the-shelf collage, and mass-produced customization.

REMODELING

The predominant method of residential reconfiguration is remodeling. As in new construction, architects are involved in only about 2% of such projects in the United States. While remodeling does result in a reconfiguration of space and structure, it is not a truly reconfigurable construction system, since its components are destroyed and replaced by new ones. Architects looking to reuse building materials must face the fact that building codes and specifications generally prohibit this without detailed inspections and certifications. The cost of new materials for this type of reconfiguration (wood studs and gypsum board, commonly) is low if we do not consider the indirect environmental or life-cycle costs of these materials. We build new, non-reconfigurable buildings and demolish their parts by remodeling at great cost to the environment; 40% of the material in U.S. landfills comes from building demolition and construction. The direct cost to consumers is not small either, as most remodeling involves high-paid skilled workers.

CUSTOM SYSTEMS

Architects have developed various systems of building components from scratch. They typically consist of a frame-and-panel system and are frequently part of a larger scheme for the mass production of houses and communities. These projects, such as the Steel House and Copper House by the Bauhaus in the 1920s as well as those by the CLASP and Arcon groups in Britain during the 1950s, employ custom-manufactured components prefabricated in factories and assembled on-site. Their parts are rarely interchangeable with those from other systems, making reconfiguration difficult after the demise of the original system's production. Most custom systems sought the economy of mass production and minimum on-site labor. Frequently, this meant sacrificing adaptability to the economies of repetition and standardized plans. Far from encouraging personalization, they have tended to create monotony among standardized environments.

OFF-THE-SHELF COLLAGE

Other architects have developed flexible construction systems through the strict use of off-the-shelf building components. The overall architectural scheme in these cases must accommodate a great variety of components to assure the future adaptability of the system. (Custom systems lack this flexibility but have the advantage that they are developed with a unity among their parts in mind.) The collage of numerous components from different manufacturers poses a challenge to the architect working with off-the-shelf products. Experiments by the British architect Cedric Price during the 1970s proved that entire buildings could be produced using off-the-shelf, readymade components but also highlighted the difficulty of creating a harmonious aesthetic effect using this approach. In 1999, a group of Boston architects determined to renovate a row house using only off-the-shelf materials available through Sweet's Catalog encountered similar difficulties in both coordinating the aesthetics of and dimensioning their architectural collage.

MASS-PRODUCED CUSTOMIZATION

Emerging computer-based manufacturing processes offer a fourth possibility for reconfiguring architecture. By integrating computers into the machinery used to manufacture building components, producers hope to turn out custom-designed parts at costs comparable to those for mass-produced identical components. The computer eliminates the labor of resetting the machine mechanically for each new design element, bringing the customization of complex building parts within the budget of architects in service to the community. The potential of mass-produced customization is currently being tested in the House_n experiment at the Massachusetts Institute of Technology.

INDIVIDUALLY ADAPTABLE ENVIRONMENTS

New technologies like the computer-based machines employed in mass-produced customization, and new materials like liquid crystal panels capable of switching between transparent and opaque states, will change the face of architecture with their ability to transform environments. But young architects in service to their communities need more modest systems that allow for personalization today. For instance, Samuel Mockbee, his students, and colleagues created reconfigurable systems at low cost with their Rural Studio projects in Alabama. Pliny Fisk and Gail Vittori, co-directors of the Center for Maximum Potential Building Systems, created an inexpensive, modular structural framework of recycled steel reinforcing bars, which can accommodate continuous user adaptation for their Advanced Green Building Demonstration Home and Workplace. When the spirit of ingenuity and invention through modest means embodied in the architecture of the Rural Studio and Center for Maximum Potential Building Systems is applied to reconfigurable systems, we may see a new kind of architecture emerge that allows building users of limited resources to adapt their environments to their individual needs.

RECONFIGURING THE DESIGN PROCESS

While reconfigurable construction systems can enable users to personalize their environments after they move in, they also have the potential to create a new kind of design process. Currently, change during the design and construction phases is discouraged because of the rework required by the architect and contractor. The cost of change during construction has been estimated at $60 billion per year in the United States. How much of this could be saved, and how many design improvements made, if we had construction systems that accommodated change during the construction process? This is already occurring in the realm of product manufacturing, where for over a decade the

House_n incorporates building components made with computer-integrated manufacturing techniques.

A modular framework of recycled steel reinforcing bars accommodates continuous user adaptation at the Advanced Green Building demonstration Home and Workplace.

tenets of concurrent engineering have offered strategies for simultaneous design and construction. Manufacturing also leads the way in considering adaptability and reuse of products as defined by the movement to design for disassembly. But in architecture, the implementation of ideas like continuous design improvement during the construction process and individually adaptable environments depend on construction systems that permit reconfiguration by both architects and users.

Construction systems should encourage participation in design and redesign by end users. They should do so with an eye not only for up-front costs, but also life-cycle costs, including repair and maintenance. Traditional construction methods such as light wood frame may currently offer the best prospects for reconfigurability because of their low cost relative to custom systems and their familiarity to the end user. However, just as computer technology continues to empower more users every day, mass-produced customization may soon provide an affordable kit of parts for the 98% without architects. High-tech or grassroots reconfigurable construction systems can move our building culture beyond the misconception that affordability and adaptability require uniformity of use toward a future wherein individual expression is an integral part of the built world.

DIRECT-TO-YOU
KRISTINE J. RENNER WADE

How can architect and client share the decisions in a design process? One model uses the concept of "shared expertise" in which each brings complementary but equally important information to the process to inform the results.

KRISTINE J. RENNER WADE was a VISTA member for one year working with Design Corps. During her year of service she secured affordable mortgages and provided architectural services to twelve low-income families.

Home. The very idea is a complex association of meanings connoting both a physical place and a more abstract sense of "a state of belonging." It embodies both a house and household, a dwelling and a refuge.[1] The notion of home assumes basic needs are being provided for, yet goes beyond this utilitarian role to feed, nurture, and protect the soul. The individual home is the fundamental building block that gives shape to the nature of community. These domestic spaces, when infused with human spirit, provide an intimacy and haven necessary to maintain a healthy quality of life.

[1] **Witold Rybczynski, *Home: A Short History of an Idea* (New York: Penguin Books, 1987), 62.**

THE FIRST MEETING

A "Direct-to-You design" group meeting, Gettysburg, Pennsylvania.

I had been preparing for several weeks for the evening's first workshop. I had posted the flyers for the housing meeting, placed the ads inviting all to come, and forwarded the press releases announcing the new program to the local gazettes. Now here I waited, shivering in the late fall evening, locked outside the Hanover, Pennsylvania, YMCA, inside which I was supposed to be hosting the initial meeting of a homeownership workshop series. After thirty minutes of stomping my feet in an effort to ward off the night's chill, when I could not possibly shove my hands any deeper into my coat pockets, I suggested to the few motley souls who had gathered that we head to the nearest eatery promising warmth. We tromped across Summit Avenue and into a local coffee shop, where we promptly ordered a round of hot drinks. As we shuffled around and settled in, I had a moment to survey the small but diverse gathering around me. Two women engulfed in recollections of the day sat across from me; to their left, a young Middle Eastern couple waited, silent and expectant. A small, timid woman hushed her children at the far end of the table, while next to me another couple, their youth betrayed in their eager countenances, spoke with my coworker about the twins they were expecting next spring. It was here that my education as an architect, as a placemaker, began to find meaningful direction.

It has long disturbed me that, in our age of customization and individualism, our housing continues to be a monotonous repetition of standardized decorated boxes. We have surrounded ourselves with a sprawling, useless "geography of nowhere," as James Howard Kunstler so accurately described our present practice of creating no-places.[2] I discovered that many are unaware of the impact the designed environment has on the quality of life. Others simply settle for suburban *sub*-standardization. Still others cannot afford the benefits of good design. The goal of serving this population spawned the initial development of the Direct-to-You design program, a process intended to provide the benefits of architecture in the form of affordable homes for the underserved.[3]

[2] **James Howard Kunstler, *The Geography of Nowhere* (New York: Simon & Schuster, 1993), 246.**

[3] **The program's name comes from a gas station in Gettysburg, Pennsylvania, that the locals referred to with familiarity as "direct-to-you gas." The premise of the program's founders is a basic notion that good design is about consideration, not cost, and the benefits of good design should be for all.**

DEFINING DIRECT-TO-YOU

When James and Missy entered our small, stark office, I immediately recognized them as the couple who had spoken excitedly about their anticipation of twins. The young couple had attended our homeownership workshops faithfully, and now eagerly, and not without some

4 We had to defend our design services to our umbrella organization, which sponsored programs as varied as Head Start and food pantries and failed to embrace our belief in the positive implications of good design on the quality of life. Thus, when partnering with a broader organization, it is important to agree on the priority of good design in both shaping the built environment and providing for the unique needs of individuals.

5 Most who participate in the Direct-to-You design process, indeed the very clients we most desire to serve, are not able to pay for the services we offer. Thus, we have promoted creative funding options such as the Federal Home Loan Bank's Affordable Housing Program, which provides up to $3500 per home in grant money. Another option to generating affordable fees is to be paid by the general contractor, which means that the design fee is rolled into the mortgage. This way the client does not have to pay a fee and retainer up front; instead a few dollars are added to each mortgage payment. Financing options such as these allow people at 50% median income to afford services such as Direct-to-You design and benefit from the attention architects can offer.

disbelief, had chosen to participate in the Direct-to-You design opportunity. I congratulated my anxious clients, calming their worries and answering their questions. I explained that nonprofits like ours often provide housing for lower-income individuals and families. Yet most nonprofits are not equipped with the design awareness or the necessary related skills to do so adequately.[4] Architects, on the other hand, have an understanding and ability to help individuals discover their needs and express their desires in built form. This process, I clarified to them, is the Direct-to-You service, which, beyond design expertise, also offers creative funding options, making good design affordable.[5] I sent them off with a booklet of information on homeownership alternatives and a questionnaire meant to gather more information concerning their housing needs. I was left with an excited anticipation of the profound opportunity I now had to participate in a home-making process with this young couple, to contribute to the shaping of a sacred space in which they would soon nurture the twins they eagerly awaited.

Direct-to-You design realizes that architecture is an intensely collaborative medium and that there is a great need to break down barriers between professionals, nonprofits, design students, and potential clients. It is a design process that seeks to both educate society and be educated by those it serves. The process acknowledges that the client has an expertise that is essential to the designing of sustainable, appropriate structures. Direct-to-You design seeks to provide an opportunity for individuals to discover ideas and ideals they hold valuable and to render them in built form. The process is a continuous exchange of information, beginning with a questionnaire designed to gain a thorough understanding of the lifestyle needs of each individual client. This provides an opportunity for the client to realize they are the expert on their needs and priorities, and good design can help accommodate these desires. Issues of activity, environment, and lifestyle are all addressed and explored. Items discussed include dining, cooking, working habits, social activities, exterior activities, religious activities, furnishings, and sleeping patterns, to name a few. Through the process of completing and discussing the questionnaire, boundaries between client and architect are dissolved, and ideals and priorities regarding domestic space are defined.

SHAPING THE PLAN

The couple returned several weeks later, Missy revealing the growth of their twins in her blossoming figure. Their completed questionnaire, dog-eared and crumpled, was accompanied by several pages torn from a home-decorating magazine. Missy really liked the cathedral ceiling in the photograph, and the fireplace would make the living room so much warmer. Would it be possible . . . maybe? And John has this gigantic fish tank—what to do with that? From our discussions, an idea of home began to take shape. To further explore

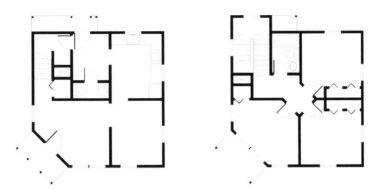

The Sosnas are a Muslim couple and their house design, which resulted through the five-meeting design program, responds spatially and in compass orientation to their ritual of prayer.

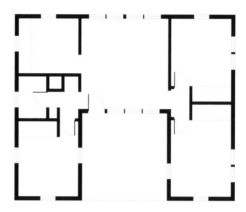

This house, for a cherry picker and his family in central Pennsylvania, draws its form from the tarps used to collect the cherries during harvest.

the possible relationships between spaces, I used simple bubble diagrams to graphically describe how spaces may be associated. These simple illustrations are easy to understand and provide an opportunity for the client to contribute in a graphic manner that is not intimidating

—anyone can draw bubbles! Try it, I encouraged them both. Initially, these bubbles simply represented activities and their relationships; however, as the design process and discussion continued, the diagrams began to connote spaces with allotted square footage numbers. Designating and distributing square footage is a challenging aspect of the process in which the client must make decisions about what is important. This is when the realities of finances come to play. Allocating square feet is equivalent to allocating dollars, and becomes a matter of prioritizing and budgeting.

Design Corps fellow Krisztina Tokes designing a house with the Solis family.

At this point in the design process, the home began to take shape. At the fourth meeting with Missy and James, I presented a series of alternative floor plans, three-dimensional models, and computer renderings. In each design, I strove to go beyond the utilitarian needs of the client, to reflect the unique dignity and spirit of the couple. Ideally, every project will become a distinct historical archive, a temple to the individual ideals, patterns, and daily activities of the client.

BENEFITS OF DIRECT-TO-YOU

I have been most challenged and most rewarded working directly with clients. Sometimes the benefits of my efforts were appreciated, while at other times what I had to offer was

Hersman house designed by Kristine J. Renner Wade, James Hersman, and Missy Hersman.

refused. During the Direct-to-You design process, I found myself facing the challenge of convincing my clients that the typical house of familiar suburban subdivisions was not always the answer to their needs. However, the alternatives I proposed were not always so readily accepted. In fact, to my naive surprise, unique designs catering to the needs of individuals were often looked upon with a great bit of suspicion, and I often found myself defending a design to the very person it was meant to serve. Direct-to-You design and its participants taught me that careful listening to the unique needs and valid opinions of each client is a necessity of good design. There exists an undeniable link between behavior and built form, and it should be the role of the architect to give such forms a shape that speaks to and sustains the spirit of the individuals who inhabit them.

The Direct-to-You design process seeks to positively reform architectural practice into a service-oriented profession. The architect becomes more than a solitary designer, taking on the role of artist, builder, interpreter, activist, and, most importantly, community member. This success is measured in client satisfaction and is based solely on the opinions given by the families Direct-to-You design is meant to serve. We give each client another questionnaire at the conclusion of the design process, in which we survey the families about the design process, their comfort level in contributing to and shaping the process, their feelings of mutual respect, and their ultimate satisfaction with the choices made based on budget and other constraints. While most of the Direct-to-You participants chose to remain anonymous in post-occupancy surveys, we made high marks across the chart, receiving unanimous support and satisfaction. So, when Missy described with eager anticipation the home in which she would soon raise her twins, and John spoke with pride of the stability his new house would provide for his boys, I considered the Direct-to-You process a success.

I believe community development organizations need programs such as Direct-to-You design that allow architects to take on a role of advocacy. Architects need to be a part of the entire development process, committing to community building on the local level, seeking local solutions to local problems extending all the way to the individual. Direct-to-You design seeks to achieve just that end, encouraging individuals to take responsibility and ownership of their built environment by infusing their own meaning into it. The Direct-to-You design process also encourages architects to seek out and accept the realities of real people, and celebrate the place-making and home-making opportunities to be found when striving to give form to the unsung nobility in the lives of those who are most often neglected and overlooked.

TIMELY TACTICS: THE STRATEGIC ROLE OF PARTICIPATION IN COMMUNITY DESIGN

MICHAEL RIOS

Strategic participation—the use of citizen involvement to build a base of local power and support, produce a project identity, and attract resources for project implementation—is an integral part of community-based design. This essay describes how design practitioners utilized this process to create a new waterfront park in the Fruitvale District of Oakland, California.

MICHAEL RIOS is assistant professor of architecture and landscape architecture at The Pennsylvania State University, director of the Hamer Center for Community Design Assistance, and president of the Association for Community Design. At the Unity Council, he was project leader for the Union Point Park project.

Participatory design is gaining prominence in design education and is being practiced by numerous organizations and individuals in the public and private sectors alike. Over 30% of North American architecture schools run university-based community design and research centers that engage the public in decision-making about the built environment.[1] Today, community designers deal with issues ranging from urban brownfield redevelopment to suburban sprawl to migrant farmworker housing. The recent upsurge in this activity raises the question, what constitutes community and in what ways can the public participate in the design process?

This essay presents the case of Union Point Park to offer a view of participatory design within a larger network of social organizations that includes community, private, educational, and government institutions. Imbedded in this form of participation are short-term actions, or tactics, that capitalize on the timing of opportunities throughout the design process.[2] The participants in these actions are not chosen randomly. Their identity and presence ensure political strength while helping to attract resources for implementation. Lessons learned from this experience suggest a vital role for design practitioners as enablers to ensure public benefits in the design of contested space.

[1] John M. Cary, Jr., *ACSA Sourcebook of Community Design Programs* (Washington, D.C.: ACSA Press, 2000).

[2] My definition of these terms are derived from Michel de Certeau's discussion of strategies and tactics in his book, *The Practice of Everyday Life* (Berkeley and Los Angeles: University of California Press, 1984), 34–39.

ORGANIZING FOR ENVIRONMENTAL CHANGE

Beginning in the early 1990s, a group of residents in the Fruitvale District of Oakland began organizing to clean up local parks overrun with trash, drugs, and other social problems. By 1995, they helped to form a community partnership called the Fruitvale Recreation and Open Space Initiative (FROSI) to address park disparity issues in this ethnically diverse section of the city. With little over half an acre of open space per 1,000 residents, the Fruitvale and adjacent San Antonio districts have the smallest amount of parks and open space in Oakland—roughly one-sixth of the standard adopted by the city. These two districts also have some of the highest concentrations of youth under the age of eighteen.

Around the same time that FROSI was formed, the public agencies The City of Oakland and The Port of Oakland had begun an ambitious planning process to reconnect Oakland's neighborhoods with its historic waterfront. The process provided FROSI an opportunity to lobby for a waterfront park at a site called Union Point. To this end they collected three thousand signatures and one hundred letters of support from citizens and community-based and nonprofit organizations. As a result of this demonstration of public support, the City and Port of Oakland agreed to work together with FROSI and develop a park at Union Point. The site was dedicated for park use, and the Unity Council, a local community development corporation, received a grant from the California Coastal Conservancy to lead a process to design Union Point Park.

REPERTOIRES OF PARTICIPATORY DESIGN

As the team leader of FROSI, I assembled a group of artists, architects, and landscape architects to work on Union Point Park. I also coordinated a group of community organizers including the Unity Council, the City of Oakland Parks Department, the Trust for Public Land (a national nonprofit organization), and the University/Oakland Metropolitan Forum, an outreach unit of the University of California, Berkeley. FROSI devised a variety of methods and techniques to solicit input from community members; these ranged from slide show presentations and visual surveys to guided walking tours and design workshops. We used the input of over five hundred residents to create a list of priorities to include in the design of Union Point Park. For example, working with community organizers and neighborhood youth, we organized sixty local teens in a charette that included a walking tour, boat ride, and an interactive design exercise using scale models of the park site. The results of this interactive workshop were synthesized into a design program that, along with information provided by surveys, established the primary elements of the park design.

FROSI relied on community patronage and advocacy to create events that both showed public support for the park and provided opportunities to interact with the site. Tapping into a network of public agencies and community organizations, we recruited partners to help shape an Earth Day celebration at Union Point. Food, music, and dance performances by local youth groups drew people to attend. Together with community organizations and public agencies, we set up educational displays, organized activities for youth, and coordinated event logistics.

At another level, the partnership that formed around the park served as a sounding board for design ideas and helped to secure political guarantees and public resources for implementation of the project. Several members of FROSI facilitated day-to-day responsibilities of partnership activities. Tasks ranged from raising grant funds to securing regulatory approvals to communicating the significance of the park's design to project partners.

BUILDING A BASE

Participation in design needs to serve multiple objectives and allow for flexibility to respond to unforeseen challenges and opportunities. In the case of Union Point Park, citizen participation was used to build a base of local power and support, create a project identity as a grassroots-driven project, and attract resources for project implementation.

Since the park's waterfront site had no immediate constituency, FROSI had to create a base of community support. We focused on the neighborhoods near the park site and then the larger Fruitvale District. We developed a work plan for the campaign and distributed information packets. We defined a single goal of securing land for park development—a difficult task given that the port owned the land and would receive minimal financial gain from using it as a park. We then supported our effort by collecting demographic information and park-related statistics about the immediate neighborhood. We provided additional information showing the benefit of a new waterfront park at Union Point. It was important for us to define the campaign in simple terms and discuss issues in ways that would resonate with a diverse population.

After our campaign of collecting and distributing data to the general community, we began to focus on elected officials. Delegations of community members met with city council members to promote our cause. This was followed by a flurry of phone calls from residents asking politicians for their support. We ensured the success of our campaign by attending highly visible events, involving the media in our efforts, and encouraging community advocacy.

Collectively, our efforts helped to build trust, cooperation, and a sense of solidarity among the participants, which grew to include community groups from the Fruitvale and adjacent San Antonio districts; Asian, Latino, and African-American organizations; youth groups; schools; and churches. These associations collected petitions, cosponsored events, and organized people to attend public meetings. FROSI established new networks with a variety of nonprofit organizations throughout the city including civic clubs and environmental,

TOP LEFT: Residents provide feedback during an Earth Day celebration at the Union Point site. TOP RIGHT: Local youth participate in a charette to create design concepts for the park. ABOVE: Phase 1 of Union Park will provide a multifunctional setting for diverse users including children, teens, and seniors.

The nine-acre site provides the only major public waterfront access for Fruitvale and San Antonio residents.

public health, and youth development groups. Each organization may have supported the project for a different reason, but each concluded that a new park was needed for the community. This provided a broad base of support that was now ready to participate in future events, activities, and decision-making associated with Union Point Park.

CREATING A PROJECT IDENTITY

FROSI worked to frame the project as a community-driven effort in a parallel organizing strategy. This involved the project team participating in citywide forums such as the Waterfront Coalition, a monthly meeting where waterfront issues were discussed. People with a diversity of interests attended these meetings to network, provide information, and discuss projects. FROSI made presentations to the Waterfront Coalition periodically to provide updates, to solicit feedback, and to frame issues related to the Union Point Park. Many such forums were eager to lend their support to our project given the poor track record of the Port of Oakland regarding citizen participation. Prior to the Estuary Plan, a joint planning initiative of the City and Port of Oakland to improve the waterfront, the port did not actively engage the broader public to discuss port policy and waterfront development issues.

Another strategy that helped to promote a unique identity was to frame the project around youth concerns. We used several activities to link the project to youth empowerment: an environmental youth summit, articles written about youth participants in local newspapers, and the presence of youth at press conferences and public meetings. At one of the press events a high-school teenager, who represented the youth participants, gave an impassioned speech about the need for a new park. She captured the attention of the California State Assembly Speaker, who later invited her to testify before a state senate subcommittee regarding a state bond to fund parks that subsequently passed.

ATTRACTING RESOURCES

One of the biggest challenges FROSI faced early on was the lack of funding for constructing the park. Some community members were at first reluctant to join us because of this. Fortunately, the California Coastal Conservancy stepped in to provide initial funding for the park's master plan. The high level of community support for the project and the clear need for waterfront access along this stretch of the shoreline were important to the conservancy's decision to join the partnership.

Community participation at events was also critical in attracting state funds for park construction. We invited state and city officials to meet community members and give speeches to them, and we acknowledged them for their leadership in supporting the project. The Earth Day celebration and community rally at Union Point was particularly helpful in attracting elected and appointed officials. Here they were able to experience the site firsthand and meet people participating in the project. State political leaders who wanted to showcase the need for urban parks cited our work in announcing their support for a major park bond measure. This helped to put Union Point Park on a short list of priority projects at both the state and city levels and led to FROSI receiving $1.5 million to fund the initial phase of park development.

MEASURABLE OUTCOMES

The master plan for Union Point Park was completed in 1999, and funding has been secured to build the first phase of the park. The project has moved into design development and the production of construction documents. Though the original design team is no longer involved with the project, the original concept, including the community's design elements, remain. The active engagement of design professionals from the early stages of the project has contributed to an exceptionally high-quality design that ensured the integration of community needs and concerns.

The project can be considered a success in its use of participatory design as a vehicle for collective action and a means to secure resources for project implementation. The project involved hundreds of local residents in a decision-making process; many became involved in their community for the first time. However, it has taken a long time to move from one phase of the project to another, due in part to the highly visible nature of the project. This has added significant costs to the project and pushed groundbreaking back several years. Partners have come and gone and grassroots community involvement has dissipated.

Despite these delays, the project continues to move forward. It is important not to lose sight of the fact that Union Point Park would not have existed without the community's will to create its own vision—a future that will provide the only major public access to Fruitvale and San Antonio's waterfront and double the amount of open space in an area that is terribly underserved.

PARTICIPATORY DESIGN AS SOCIAL PRACTICE

The experience of creating Union Point Park illustrates the important role that participatory design plays in contributing to local mobilizing efforts. Citizen involvement created political support, framed issues, and secured resources for project implementation. At times, we viewed the community as a client whose purpose was to provide feedback on the park design. During other phases of the project, the community articulated its own ideas for the park, and we served in a facilitating role between different interests, organizations, and agencies. By combining the strategic participation of both individual residents and community organizations with different repertoires of techniques and methods, we accomplished our project goals.

How is a project like Union Point Park useful to participatory design? First, it suggests a role for architects beyond professional design assistance. It shows that skills in group facilitation and community organizing are equally important. Second, it demonstrates how an awareness of larger political processes can help to position a project in order for it to receive support and secure resources. Capitalizing on political opportunities and the unique contributions of local residents and organizations can go a long way in accomplishing project tasks. Lastly, it advocates that architects and landscape architects are in a unique position to serve as catalysts for community empowerment and social change. Successful participatory design requires an ability to move across disciplinary and epistemological boundaries, from community organizing to design, from expert knowledge to local wisdom. An ability to grasp these dimensions of place-making in communities can serve to deepen the practice of participatory design.

MAKING A STUDIO PROJECT REAL
VICTORIA BALLARD BELL

Can community-based design be initiated and completed within an academic setting? This essay shows what students can do, and what critical pieces are left to be completed outside of the semester schedule.

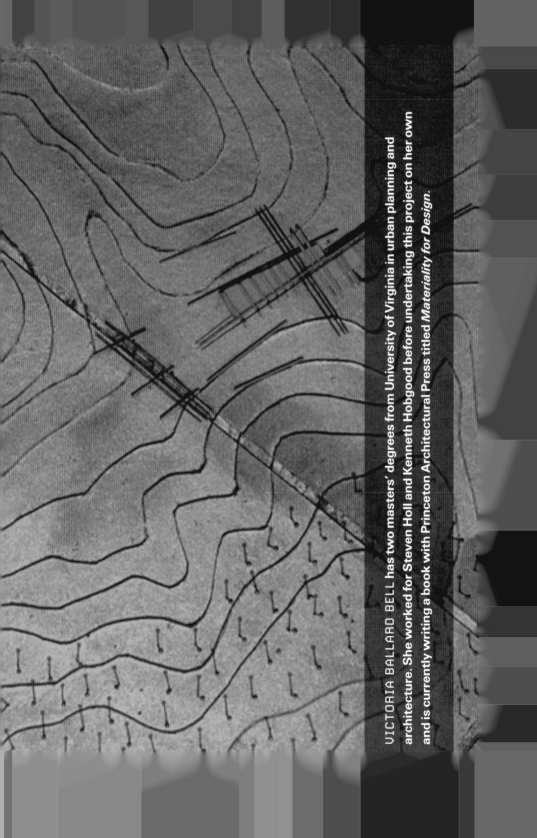

VICTORIA BALLARD BELL has two masters' degrees from University of Virginia in urban planning and architecture. She worked for Steven Holl and Kenneth Hobgood before undertaking this project on her own and is currently writing a book with Princeton Architectural Press titled *Materiality for Design*.

The Marion Child-Care and Technology Training Center began as an academic project in a University of Virginia architecture studio taught by Samuel "Sambo" Mockbee in 1997. Eleven of us graduate students were fortunate enough to be involved in this studio. Each student visited the city of Marion, in Perry County, Alabama, spoke with residents and representatives, and completed a design proposal for the project.

The program evolved during the semester to help the local unemployed and underemployed increase their earnings. The program was developed at a time when many families were moving from "welfare to work," and Marion residents lacked both the necessary job training and childcare to make quality work possible. The project provided one solution to both problems: one building that would house the two needed services. Training in the technology sector was particularly needed because the residents had been left behind in the industrial age and did not want to be left behind again in the cyber age.

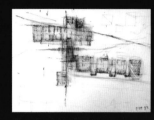

First sketch for the design.

Our conversations with the community involved not only these functional requirements but also the aesthetics and the symbolism of the proposed building. Community members expressed a strong opinion that this building should represent "the bold and new, and a sign of the future." A strong pride of place, history, and heritage notwithstanding, there was less interest in the vernacular look made familiar by the rusted metal aesthetic of Mockbee's Rural Studio, located nearby in Newbern. The local consensus was that the new building should propel the community into the twenty-first century.

At the final jury of our design proposals, three community leaders—the mayor and two local activists—were present to help assess the results. The studio project gave the town the opportunity to have the energies and talents of design students focused on their needs, and offered the students a rare chance to have a real client.

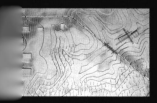

e model showing Marion, Alabama,
ustrial park and proposed center.

BEYOND THE STUDIO

But how real was the project? After the studio ended, the project did not move forward. Although Marion was in favor of the project and had contributed to creating the program, there was no one there to shepherd the project forward from the design stage. Someone would need to acquire funds for the building, gathering additional local input, and face all the other real issues that architecture entails.

One year after the studio ended, nothing further had happened on the project. Knowing the reality of Marion's need and the sincerity that the community brought to the proposal, I felt that this plan should not be ignored and forgotten. My enthusiasm for making this project happen was strengthened by visiting the Rural Studio for some juries. My first step toward restarting the project was to call the mayor of Marion, Edward Daniel, and ask if he wanted to proceed; his answer was an enthusiastic yes. This turned out to be the kind of proactive move needed in this situation. Nobody gave me permission to do this, but I was correct to think that otherwise the project was dead. Taking this step made the critical leap from the studio to reality (although one phone call was not all that was required). This is the essence of serving the underserved: for many reasons, they do not call us; we have to make the call and offer to help.

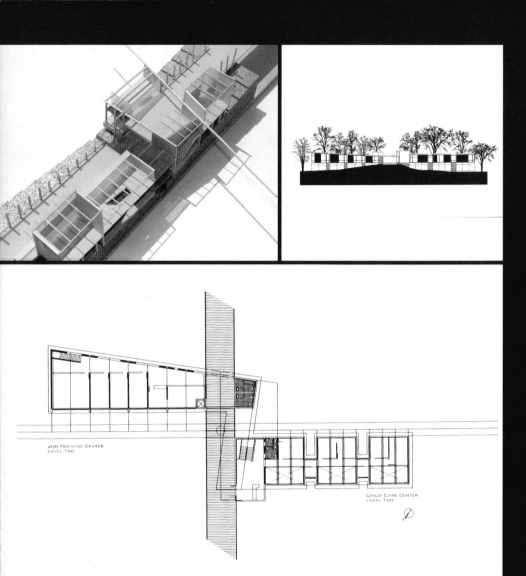

TOP LEFT: Sectional model showing both child-care and job-training centers. TOP RIGHT: North elevation. ABOVE: Second floor plan.

FUNDING THE PROJECT

The next step was to look for funding sources for the $1.2 million project. Since most grants require a nonprofit organization as an applicant, Design Corps, a nonprofit design firm, agreed to play this role. We identified a federal program called the Rural Housing and Economic Development Program, which the Department of Housing and Urban Development (HUD) had recently started. Seth Peterson, a Volunteers in Service to America (VISTA) participant with Design Corps and also a UVA graduate, helped me write the grant. We worked to make the building more efficient and economical, a task we had not faced in the studio.

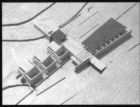

One of many study models.

To put the grant together and refine the project, we began working with the Perry County Chamber of Commerce and the Sowing Seeds of Hope Initiative of the Southern Baptists, a large group with early roots in Marion. Together, these two organizations provided a structure for holding meetings and assembling a team for input and support from the area. The team started collecting data that would form the basis for the grant request.

Grant writing is very effective at grounding a project in reality. Funders look for how the proposed project will meet the needs of the community, the effectiveness of the proposed solution, the ability of the applicant to deliver what has been proposed, and a realistic budget. Working these questions out while refining the design is the type of experience that is lacking in architecture schools or in the responsibilities interns usually receive at their first jobs. In fact, tackling key issues—What is the best site? What is the program? What is the budget?—gave the design team greater input into the choices usually made by others. Since we were seeking the funds, we were as realistic as we could be about these choices.

To establish need, a statistician from Marion's Judson College created a child-care questionnaire that the local Family Resources Center distributed at its office. It was difficult to get a sufficient number of responses, but eventually we gathered forty. In our grant essay, we presented other statistics as well (for example, Perry County has the second highest rate of poverty in the state, for both adults and children).

One challenge in preparing the grant was to match our solution with the goals of the federal (HUD) program. Since the proposed center was neither housing nor traditional "economic development" (which means job creation), we needed to show that daycare would enable single mothers to enter the workforce and that technology training would allow residents to move from low-paying manual labor to higher-paying skilled jobs. We needed to prove that the presence of the dual-purpose center in the community could actually attract new businesses by offering training and child-care for their employees.

Putting the budget together took some guesswork. After several design reviews by the team, we were able to get the size and budget within a realistic range. This was an important lesson. Architects can make idealistic but naive proposals that create problems for others. It is easy to propose a space for child-care or classrooms for training, but it takes local long-term support to staff and run these facilities. In fact, the cost to run this dual-purpose center would be much greater than the cost of construction. Without addressing both—construction and operating costs—the project had no real chance of success.

It was critical to learn about the specific requirements of the HUD program. The maximum amount funded for one project was $400,000, so it would have been a mistake to ask for more.

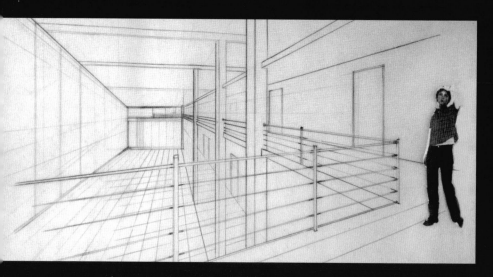

Perspective sketch from the child-care center overlooking classrooms and pods below.

We had to show reasonable sources for the remaining balance. The city was donating the land and the infrastructure (sewer, water, and paving), but otherwise we had very little committed funding. Members of local colleges and Volunteers of America wrote letters of support and committed to the long-term needs of training and child-care. In fact, Judson College has an excellent early education degree, which meant the partnership could be mutually beneficial.

THE NEXT STEP

Despite the great need that was demonstrated and the teamwork employed to write the grant application, our first application was not successful. We did receive feedback on the application and learned that we had scored well in the Applicant Capacity category, but not as well in the Matching Funds category. The other categories were Need and Extent of Problem, Soundness of Approach, and Comprehensiveness and Coordination. The ranking that seemed most unfair was that we received only seventeen out of forty in the Need and Extent of Problem category.

All was not lost. I reapplied to HUD in 2002 with that feedback in mind, was successful, and have been funded for the full $400,000 requested. I also applied for funding from the National Endowment of the Arts for the Arts Design Access program, which could pay for remaining architectural fees. This grant was also funded and will provide $40,000 for design fees.

The support for the project in the community is strong. In fact, seven groups including two local colleges and the Retired Teachers Association have together pledged $220,000 per year to operate the center. It is good to know that there is the support to make this happen and to help make a project like this become reality.

Perhaps the most important lesson I learned is that persistence—from calling the mayor to writing and rewriting grants—is required to make a community design project a reality. While I am using the skills I learned in school, I am learning how to implement a process to reach the construction stage. If the goal is providing the benefits of design to the underserved, then the benefits of design are only realized when a design is built.

2 / TUNING ESTABLISHED MODELS

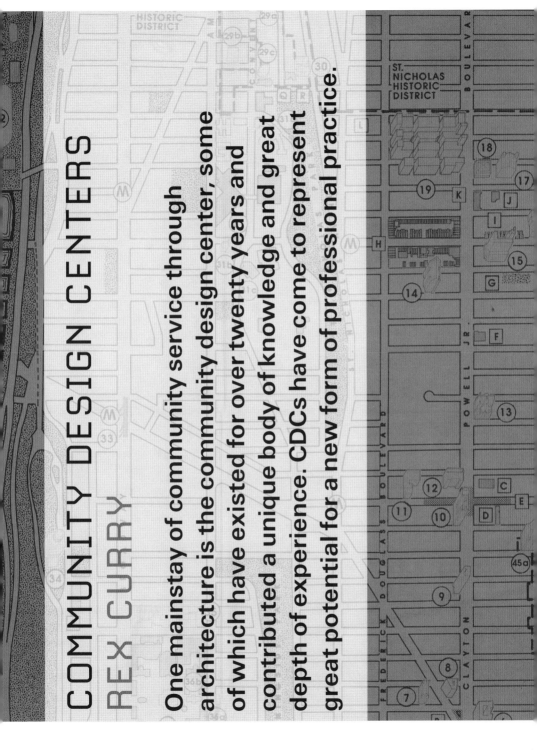

COMMUNITY DESIGN CENTERS

REX CURRY

One mainstay of community service through architecture is the community design center, some of which have existed for over twenty years and contributed a unique body of knowledge and great depth of experience. CDCs have come to represent great potential for a new form of professional practice.

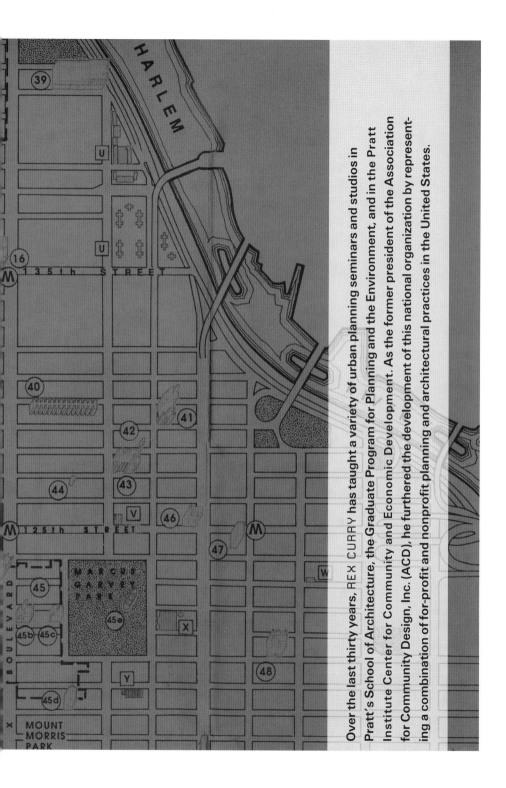

Over the last thirty years, REX CURRY has taught a variety of urban planning seminars and studios in Pratt's School of Architecture, the Graduate Program for Planning and the Environment, and in the Pratt Institute Center for Community and Economic Development. As the former president of the Association for Community Design, Inc. (ACD), he furthered the development of this national organization by representing a combination of for-profit and nonprofit planning and architectural practices in the United States.

Just over thirty years ago, at the one-hundredth convention of the American Institute of Architects in Portland, Oregon, Whitney M. Young, Jr., demanded more accountability from the architectural profession. He indicated that inner cities were in great distress, and the architectural profession was not rising to the challenge of addressing their physical and social problems. His concern remains today, but it has been met in part by an idea that emerged at this meeting—the community design center (CDC). Through CDCs, architects and planners have found creative ways to serve community organizations and distressed urban and rural regions throughout the country. CDCs have contributed to two new social empowerment goals: valuing neighborhood and community leadership as essential to lasting, useful social change, and creating alternative markets for investment. Young strongly suggested that universities could lead the way by nurturing a new and diverse base of talent that could alter the profession's dependency on market forces and focusing on helping communities meet their needs.

I will describe some of the lessons I have learned over the last thirty years at the Pratt Institute Center for Community and Environmental Development (PICCED) and from many colleagues who supported the continuing development of the national Association for Community Design (ACD).[1] In this way I will share my perspective about the successes and challenges to the institutionalization of CDCs.

CONTINUOUS LEARNING RELATIONSHIPS

Paulo Freire, in *Pedagogy of the Oppressed*, defined an authentic educational experience:

> Authentic help means that all who are involved help each other mutually, growing together in common effort to understand the reality which they seek to transform. Only through such praxis—in which those who help and those who are being helped help each other simultaneously—can the act of helping become free from the distortion in which the helper dominates the helped.[2]

[1] CDCs are defined at http://www.communitydesign.org in the *History of Community Design* "About Us" section. Contributions to the site are always welcome.

[2] Paulo Freire, *Pedagogy of the Oppressed*, 20th anniversary edition (New York: Continuum, 1996), 136.

Based on this idea, the university and the community share the responsibility of enriching the student-faculty educational experience and participating in the community's development.

The traditional student-faculty experience is embedded in the fifteen-week semester. It has a central subject, a set of tasks, and routine evaluation periods. If the university wants only to enrich the faculty-student experience, this is all that is required. But if it seeks a role in community development, it needs to effectively engage the community, develop methods for assisting communities in choosing what to know, and place greater control over the content, quality, and character of the services in the hands of those served. In adapting these elements CDCs become an influential force for community development.

GOALS OF THE CDC

The Association for Community Design serves a variety of CDCs, including university-based, university-linked, independent nonprofit, and volunteer organizations that draw from professionals willing to support community development initiatives. All CDCs serve as advocates for social justice in an adversarial system of adjudication. They help to make viable arguments for resources to right past wrongs and build local capacity.

An individual architectural project has a developer, a contractor, and an end user to whom the designer is accountable. In the community design model, the whole community is

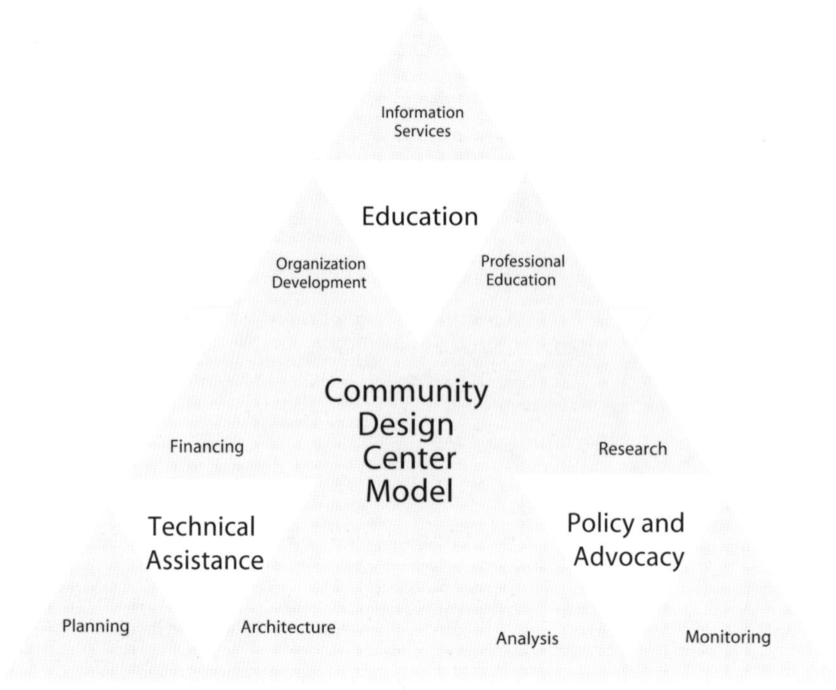

Information
Services

Education

Organization
Development

Professional
Education

Community
Design
Center
Model

Financing

Research

Technical
Assistance

Policy and
Advocacy

Planning

Architecture

Analysis

Monitoring

Diagram describing philosophical and management structure of PICCED.

considered to be the developer, contractor, and end user. This engenders an entirely differ-ent design process offering multilayered opportunities. With this vision, CDCs can respond to a project for a community garden while simultaneously regarding a multifamily, substan-tial rehabilitation project or the construction of a new child-care center.

Meeting the community on level ground means just that. How many beautifully designed playgrounds by design-build studios fell to ruin a few years later? How many new public housing projects and community facilities were built but failed to garner the resources or even recognize the need for a much larger capacity-building process? Even high-quality, award-winning designs have been failures. In my view, the missing component has been the quality of end-user control. Home ownership is on top of the list these days, as are the mutual housing and co-housing. Other forms of end-user control, such as strong ten-ant organizations and community-based management and development corporations, are equally relevant.

The CDC is a nonprofit model of service that promotes such developed ideas; however, it is more likely that the CDC advocates for something previously thought unlikely, if not impossible. When successful, they create opportunity; the for-profit firm in the community celebrates the CDC's arrival and provides it with assistance. As an old saying goes, "If you attack the establishment long and hard enough, it will eventually make you a member."

PROBLEM-BASED LEARNING

It is not always the CDC's first choice to jump right into the fray and attack the complex con-ditions that negatively alter the quality of life in a community. It is also possible for the uni-versity to offer safe haven for all concerned. In developing a working relationship between a university and a community there is a difference in the questions that define problem-based learning and service-based learning. "What problem are we trying to solve?" is quite differ-ent from "What service are we capable of providing?" The first question attempts to define the issues; the second is a take-it-or-leave-it proposition. To implement programs that are sensitive to this issue, a CDC needs to note three things: a community in socioeconomic dis-tress is not a place for class experiments; continuity with the community from semester to semester, year to year, is mandatory; and defining and redefining the problems addressed is a continuous process for all participants.

The work is a full-time job with full-time responsibilities. Community engagement processes are not limited to one-time workshops but are multiple procedures applied to shifting contexts throughout the timeframe of a community development process. Faculty and students should work and think in terms of an ordinary calendar year. They need a staffing structure that supports this framework. What an organization can make recur is a demonstration of control, stability, and accountability to these cycles of activity.

CDC MODELS

PICCED began as a vision of service to the distressed communities of New York City by architects and planners in Pratt's graduate planning department. Founded in 1963, it is the oldest university-based advocacy planning organization in the country. The graphic at left describes the philosophical and, to some degree, the management structure of PICCED.

Among its first community projects were community leadership training workshops in the 1960s and early 1970s. PICCED planners literally translated federal urban renewal legis-lation into terms people could understand and illustrated to them the probable impacts on

Robert F. Kennedy visited the Bedford-Stuyvesant community in 1966.

their home turf. PICCED's technical assistance and advocacy attempted to generate community-based alternatives to proposals developed by nonresidents. This established development concepts that reflected local values, interests, needs, and concerns.

Senator Robert F. Kennedy toured the Bedford-Stuyvesant community in 1966. In the preceding three years, a comprehensive neighborhood plan conducted by PICCED and the Central Brooklyn Coordinating Council was ongoing. Senator Kennedy's visit helped to form the consensus, and capital for the nation's first community-based development corporation— the Bedford Stuyvesant Restoration Corporation. The community's vision was to create a locally controlled community development corporation with the capacity for comprehensive and integrative development. Such partnerships with community groups in leadership development supported the provision of architectural services through faculty participation, joint ventures, and the formation of the Pratt Planning and Architectural Collaborative in the mid-1970s, at the height of New York City's housing crisis.

PICCED's focus ranges from learning though leadership training experiences to creating affordable housing through preservation and development. Without this grounding in the reality of capacity building and in the development of local nonprofit ownership and control mechanisms, PICCED's internal capacity for policy analysis and advocacy would have been weak.

With the assistance of PICCED, New York's City College Architectural Center (CCAC) was formed in 1977. It provides comprehensive planning assistance and supports joint ventures. In part, this is a lesson of the Architect's Renewal Committee of Harlem (ARCH). The lack of separation between the community empowerment agenda and the "build" agenda tends to be at the heart of local controversies and led to the loss of ARCH as a resource in Harlem. The CCAC benefited from this knowledge and did not become architects of record in the community. Instead, CCAC became a teaching office. Its services have been shaped by the partnership for learning that can occur between community organization participants and students of planning and architecture. One of CCAC's most popular products is "Landmarks of Harlem," a detailed foldout map with photos and walking tours highlighting Harlem's social and architectural history. One of the best forms of activism is recognizing the need for a resource and serving that need.

Other CDCs—in particular, the Los Angeles Community Design Center (LACDC) formed in 1968, San Francisco's Asian Neighborhood Design (AND) formed in 1973, and Seattle's Environmental Works (EW) formed in 1971—have sustained their public service mission by becoming nonprofit, regional development corporations in partnership with community leaders in distressed neighborhoods. Their demonstration projects set new standards for participation and design and their efforts capitalized on developing new businesses on behalf of their low- and moderate-income constituency. AND turned a local job-training program into a national high-end office furniture company. Its unique combination of leadership training in the formation of a nonprofit private sector company and its tenacity in getting market share in housing development and industrial design is well known.

In contrast a single-minded entrepreneurial approach can become a problem. In one case, a CDC design team beat out a member of its own board of directors for a major architectural project. This sparked a review of this CDC's mission that threatened its capacity to stay fully involved with the day-to-day problems of community development. The CDC won its demand for an empirical base in development but agreed to limit its practice to the most highly distressed areas. Another CDC spent many years building an organization in a large

Historic landmarks map by the City College Architectural Collaborative.

public housing complex, only to be challenged in court by the state's board of architects.[3] This CDC was forced to leave its university base in order to sustain its role in addressing tenant control issues regarding the rehabilitation of public housing.

Staying small works; the director of the Community Design Center in Minneapolis, formed in 1969, preferred to take on projects that illustrated the capacity of the community base to innovate on its own behalf. Its "food and fiber project" is an example of focusing on community assets. In this case, small scale home-based food packaging and garment manufacturing. Bringing planning and design to this community contributed to small business development by women. Sizing pro bono activities in relation to the market area also works. The Troy Architecture Program (TAP), formed in 1969 in Troy, New York, has sustained its nonprofit status by simply staying within the IRS rules and in so doing within the limits of the market for services in its region. The work of this office, including helping a low-income household get indoor plumbing and restoring a church basement's former glory as an after-school center, proves that a private practice career in low-income communities is possible.

An emphasis on training and education has served the remaining university CDCs that began in the 1960s and 1970s, the Louisville Community Design (1968), Assist Inc. (1969) in Salt Lake City, Utah, the East Tennessee Community Design Center (1970) in Knoxville, and the Community Design Center of Atlanta (1976). These CDCs have also remained small and focused on integrative planning and research.

Four CDC volunteer programs must also be considered for their longevity and effect. The most recognized volunteer program structure is that of the Community Design Center of Pittsburgh (CDCP), formed in 1968. In openly marketing its work as a broker of architectural and planning services, CDCP has confronted and solved many of the problems and limitations of volunteerism. It provides a mechanism for the city's major firms to seek out its assistance, experience, and in-house expertise. Its popular Renovation Information Network provides a vehicle through which demonstration projects can be managed. CDCs in Baltimore (Neighborhood Design Center, formed in 1968), Philadelphia (Community Design Collaborative, formed in 1968), and Washington, D.C. (Community Design Services, formed in 1991), with varying degrees of volunteer participation, have also sustained a mechanism that supports the engagement of architecture, engineering, and planning firms in distressed areas.

Until ACD was formed in 1975, resources to assist in the formation of CDCs and help them through tough times were rare at the local level and difficult to fund nationally. The ACD has advocated for permanent forms of public service design practices that can integrate the functions of community organizing, planning, finance, and architecture.

THE FUTURE OF CDCS

CDCs remain a somewhat silent partner in the world of design. They have not been effective chroniclers of their own times and work. As CDCs generally shift credit to their clients, they often do not assume the esteem they deserve for their work. As much of the architectural media still holds the traditional view that design is a high-value servant of the wealthy

3 The CDC's work was built on the implementation of Section 3 of the Housing and Community Development Act of 1968. It requires the local housing authority to make a best effort in building the capacity of community businesses and residents in all public investment and building rehabilitation activities. Congress established this policy to ensure economic opportunities generated by Federal assistance be directed toward low-income persons, particularly those who are recipients of government assistance for housing.

4 Arthur Mehrhoff, *Community Design: A Team Approach to Dynamic Community Systems* (London: Sage, 1999); Henry Sanoff, *Community Participation Methods in Design and Planning* (New York: John Wiley & Sons, Inc., 2000); and Nick Wates, *The Community Planning Handbook: How People Can Shape Their Cities, Towns and Villages in any Part of the World* (London: Earthscan Publications Ltd., 2000) present techniques for community participation. W. Morrish and C. Brown, *Planning To Stay* (University of Minnesota: The Design Center for American Urban Landscape, 1994) is an excellent manual for mitigating the damage of social and economic change on a neighborhood. T. Jones, W. Pettus, and M. Pyatok, *Good Neighbors: Affordable Family Housing* (New York: McGraw-Hill, 1997) includes a description of process for community participation in design.

5 *New Village: Building Sustainable Cultures* is a publication of Architects/Designers/Planners for Social Responsibility, Berkeley, California; it focuses on planning, development, and revitalization processes. *Designer/Builder: A Journal of The Human Environment* is published by Fine Additions of Santa Fe, New Mexico, and is dedicated to examining creative partnerships between organizations serving low- and moderate-income communities and the design and building professions.

and powerful, CDC design has received limited publicity, and efforts to reach out from the grassroots are few and far between. There are signs this is changing with the growing body of literature on community engagement.[4] Two relatively new periodicals, *New Village* and *Designer/Builder*,[5] are important in reestablishing a mainstream dialog on issues of social change from a planning and architectural viewpoint.

CDCs will need more than publicity to achieve balance, if not power, in the community building process. Into whose hands do we now entrust the future of a distressed community? The answer is unique to each locality. CDCs have managed to establish new fronts, but more documentation is needed to support and broaden the dialog, and to firmly establish them as valued community-development resources.

Successful community design centers are those that have encouraged community organization to solve problems by engaging in the type of helping relationship defined by Paulo Freire. An effective design center program engages learners in problem-finding and problem-solving situations that address the complexity of unmet need and weak or nonexistent economic demand for services. When working in distressed areas, design uses tools that help people understand a reality they would like to transform. Design enables the building of mutually enriching and role-reversible relationships between those who help and those who are being helped. The idea is to achieve a sustainable community building process that argues for balance and human dignity.

Imagine professional schools in a university as vertical elements without much communication between them. In this setting, the CDC might connect a neighborhood organizer's work with a community to an urban planner's research on vacant lots and a landscape architect's selection of those most suitable for gardens and playgrounds. It is helpful for the organizer to find people who would hope to create a garden and those who would seek the physicality of a playground. It is helpful for the planner to define the social demography surrounding each site in relationship to the constituency of the organizer. Infill housing, childcare, or housing could emerge as possibilities. It is helpful for the designer to have a community interested in site evaluations, site preparation work for interim uses, or design and build experiences that represent a desire for change. I believe that the lifelong act of learning how to build a community is perfected in the practice of community design.

USE OF DESIGN WITH HABITAT FOR HUMANITY
EVAN HARREL

Since 1976, Habitat for Humanity has made the opportunity of home ownership available for more than one hundred thousand families in seventy-nine nations. This essay examines the lessons from one design project for Houston Habitat for Humanity and explores where architects, planners, and Habitat could go from here to work together to erase substandard housing.

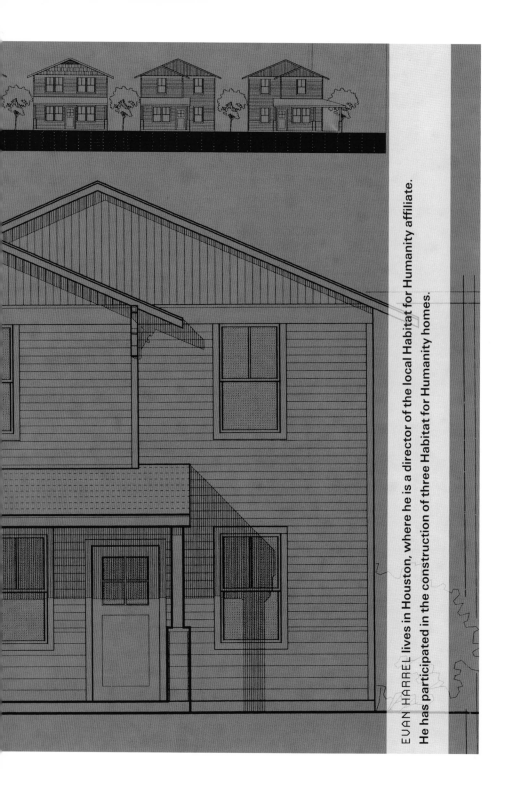

EVAN HARREL lives in Houston, where he is a director of the local Habitat for Humanity affiliate. He has participated in the construction of three Habitat for Humanity homes.

Habitat for Humanity International (HFHI) is a Christian organization dedicated to eradicating substandard housing through the development of simple, decent, affordable housing for those in need. Local Habitat affiliates work with financial donors, volunteers, and homeowners to plan, design, and build the homes. Homeowners are selected based upon their need—they must reside in substandard housing and they must meet certain income limits. In Houston in 2000, the maximum allowable family income was $23,250. Habitat homebuyers purchase their homes just like other, more traditional buyers do: with a down payment followed by mortgage payments for a typical period of twenty to thirty years. A number of elements make the Habitat home purchase affordable for low-income purchasers. First, the down payment on the home comes in the form of hundreds of hours—three hundred in Houston—of sweat equity put into the construction of their own home or toward other Habitat work. The mortgage extended by Habitat to the homeowner is interest free. Homeowners and volunteers construct the homes, thereby reducing their total cost, and Habitat sells the homes at no profit.

A Habitat home is obviously intended to address the immediate need of shelter of low-income individuals, but it must be seen in the greater context of the problems of poverty, which are manifold: high crime rates, poor education, insufficient access to healthcare and transportation, and instability in families and neighborhoods. A decent, affordable place to live can be the foundation in the battle against these ills of poverty. A number of studies have established that homeownership can have a profound impact on many elements of the homeowner's life. First-time homeowners have better feelings about themselves and are happier with their lives than renters are.[1] The children of homeowners spend more time in school and are less likely to become pregnant than children of renters.[2] The benefits of homeownership lead to economic advancement across generations, and the children of homeowners attain a higher level of education and earn more throughout their career than the children of renters.[3] They are also significantly more likely to become homeowners themselves than are the children of renters. Thus, decent, affordable housing can help address much more than just the problem of inadequate housing. It can contribute to the solution of many of the other problems experienced in poverty.

[1] William M. Rohe and Michael A. Stegman, "The Effects of Homeownership on the Self-Esteem, Perceived Control and Life Satisfaction of Low-Income People," *Journal of the American Planning Association* 60, no. 1 (April 1994): 173–84.

[2] Richard K. Green and Michelle J. White, "Measuring the Benefits of Homeowning: Effects on Children," *Journal of Urban Economics* 41, no. 3 (May 1997): 441–61.

[3] Thomas P. Boehm and Alan M. Schlottman, "Does Home Ownership by Parents Have an Economic Impact on Their Children?" *Journal of Housing Economics* 8, no. 3 (September 1999): 217–32.

Habitat's desire to address a broad range of poverty-related ills is an ambitious one. Professionals aware of the relationship between housing and the impact it can have on life are in an ideal situation to help Habitat in its ambitions. Habitat needs good designers who are sensitive to the needs of the organization and its home purchasers.

NEEDS IN A HABITAT DESIGN

Habitat is organized into over 1,900 local affiliates, which are responsible for the construction of homes and selection of Habitat homeowners. Design of a Habitat house is determined by the local affiliates subject to limitations and requirements of HFHI. Designs are typically consistent with other low-cost housing in a local market. Among the design criteria that HFHI demands of its affiliates are a maximum size (1,050 square feet for a three-bedroom house, for example), covered primary entrance, one bathroom, no garages or carports, and an options budget to help the home purchaser personalize the house. HFHI encourages the purchasing family to contribute to the design of the home as much as possible. Since Habitat relies largely on volunteer construction of its houses, the design needs to be easy to build.

Habitat limits the size of its homes for a few important reasons. The first is simply affordability, which is part of Habitat's mission. Habitat homeowners have among the lowest income of all homeowners. An additional 10% in construction costs will translate into an additional 10% in the monthly mortgage payment. This small amount may be the difference between being able to afford the payment and not.

Second, given the limited resources available to alleviate substandard housing, building more expensive houses translates into building fewer houses. A good example of this was recently described in Habitat's *Affiliate Update* magazine.[4] The South Brevard, Florida, HFHI affiliate found that the zoning regulations in Melbourne, Florida, require that all new homes be built with at least a one-car garage. This affiliate can build nine homes without a garage for the same cost it would take to build eight with a garage. In order to serve as many potential Habitat homeowners as possible, it sought variances for the homes it builds and was successful. If it had been required to build homes with garages, every ninth family Habitat currently serves would have been left behind in substandard poverty housing. So the challenge for an architect in the design of a Habitat house is to create something aesthetically pleasing that is also affordable.

[4] Kim Gabriel, "Staying True to Building Affordable Housing," *Affiliate Update* 3 (2001): 8–9.

Historically, the collaboration between Habitat and the design community has been limited. Design professionals have dismissed Habitat housing as poorly designed while Habitat builders have seen design introducing unnecessary expense and production complexity.

HOUSTON HABITAT DESIGN PROJECT

In 2000, the Houston office of the architecture firm Gensler approached Houston Habitat about sponsoring and building a Habitat house. Gensler had been named winner of the national 2000 AIA Architecture Firm Award, and as part of its celebration was seeking to return something to the local community. It was only natural that, in addition to sponsoring the house financially and providing the workers to build it, Gensler should design the house.

Architects and builders often view development through different lenses, and this project was no different. The main point of divergence was a classic one: the appropriate balance between cost and aesthetics. Gensler sought to bring their design sense to the project, while Habitat desired to limit its mission to simple, decent housing, and not to go further. As a Christian organization, Habitat's desire for simplicity is in part an issue of faith. Christ's teaching is full of lessons and stories warning against the dangers of seeking satisfaction through earthly goods.[5] The writings of the French philosopher Jean-Jacques Rousseau also explored this issue of simplicity in needs.[6] Rousseau believed that man's true needs are few in number. Among these, of course, is shelter. According to Rousseau, much of what man desires is driven by the importance man attaches to how others view him, or what Rousseau called "amour propre." In the communities served by Habitat, many basic needs are not being met at all. Habitat seeks to stay focused on these.

[5] For a comprehensive coverage of a Christian view of simplicity, see Richard J. Foster, *Freedom of Simplicity* (New York: Harper Paperbacks, 1998).

[6] Jean-Jacques Rousseau, *A Discourse on Inequality*, trans. Maurice Cranston (New York: Penguin Classic, 1984).

Gensler plan for a two-story square footprint of 24' x 24' results in 1,152 square feet of living space. Designed with a wrap-around porch with a corner lot in mind, this plan can be adapted to fit a small mid-block lot as well.

Gensler was given guidance on Habitat's design philosophy by the Houston affiliate, who shares HFHI's design requirements and limitations. It shares Habitat's mission and the need to design homes that fit that mission. As the design process continued, the parties discussed limitations on finish materials. Houston Habitat is often able to get material donated, and the organization wants to specify finish material that could potentially be donated and that is easy to maintain. The architects initially chose siding that was not the vinyl siding Houston Habitat traditionally has used. On Habitat's insistence, they agreed to change to vinyl siding, but were able to use it in different colors to achieve some of the effects they had wanted to achieve with potentially more expensive and difficult to maintain siding materials.

Three of Gensler's thirteen in-house designs were submitted to Habitat for final selection: a one-story front-loaded house with front and back porches, a one-story house side-loaded through a courtyard, and a two-story house with all living areas downstairs and sleeping areas upstairs. The designs were evaluated by Habitat on several criteria. Is the design volunteer friendly? Is it timeless and not dated? How does the project relate to the outside? Is there the potential to add a second bathroom? Are there distinctive elements, and what are they? Is it within a budget of about $50,000? Is it able to have variations? How does it look in a group?

The two-story house was selected as the winner. Some of the comments about the scheme were:

Two-story requires scaffolding, safety equipment, and lift equipment to get trusses to second floor. Need to explore liability issues.

Probably within budget. Tradeoff between smaller slab versus extra trusses for two-story construction.

Good porches create community feel.

Distinctive lines.

Suggest nine-foot first floor, eight-foot second floor.

Looks good in a group setting.

Some of the comments about the other two finalists, which would also be accepted into Habitat's working plans, were:

Like front and back porch. Kitchen does not overlook play area.

Side-loaded more efficient in using outdoor space, but overall design is introverted.

Similar to our current design.

Lines are modernistic, not classic.

Volunteer friendly, but involves trusses for cathedral ceiling.

The selected design was built in mid-2001 and was received well by the purchaser and her neighbors. Many people appreciated its uniqueness as a two-story house—the first two-story house that Houston Habitat has built. Construction was more difficult than for Habitat's traditional one-story houses, but this complexity was not a stumbling block for this specific project. Many of the volunteers were construction professionals, which minimized problems. Houston Habitat has had very good support from the local home building community, and construction professionals have sponsored and/or built many of its homes. This house may be too difficult for a crew of nonprofessionals, but the affiliate should be able to continue to build it using more experienced crews.

WHERE TO GO FROM HERE

Houston Habitat has been an extremely fortunate recipient of some exceptional design work. The affiliate has three new floor plans, two of which have already been built, which diversify the pool of potential designs. The more designs available to Habitat, the easier it will be to involve the homeowners in this important decision that will shape their lives. The collaboration with Gensler was successful because of the architects' sensitivity to this nonprofit builder's needs: low cost, volunteer friendliness, and aesthetic and construction material limitations. The project has the potential to lead to even greater change due to the dialog that it has generated.

Design dialog can get lost among the many significant challenges of a nonprofit builder. The first job for most organizations is funding. For Houston Habitat, the most difficult task in recent years has been acquiring land. It is also responsible for selecting and nurturing families, recruiting volunteers, and, of course, constructing homes. As all of these duties consume limited time and resources, design can seem to be a luxury for many in the nonprofit world. The collaboration between Habitat and Gensler revealed that it is not. Thoughtful design can be a central element in the mission of nonprofit builders. Habitat knows that homeownership improves the measures of life for the homeowner, especially for those in substandard housing. Intentional design can further these improvements in the quality of life.

The challenge has been, and will likely continue to be, to get architects and nonprofit builders to talk the same language. Habitat knows what it wants to build: simple, decent, and easy-to-construct housing. This must be the jumping-off point in the dialog with architects. Of course, as with much in the nonprofit sector, finding the resources and leadership to address design needs will always be a hurdle. The need is there for superior design in the nonprofit sector. For those interested in responding to this need, a range of roles including providing funding, participating in designing and building, and advocating for the value of design will all help achieve this goal.

SORE SHOULDERS, BRUISED ETHICS: THE UNINTENDED LESSONS OF DESIGN-BUILD

SCOTT WING

While nonprofit housing organizations, such as Habitat for Humanity, create thousands of units every year, their role as decision makers can be an issue when quality in design becomes a goal. Local nonprofits have knowledge of local problems and needs, and well-established community relationships, but can they become interference in the direct design relationship between a family and the designers?

SCOTT WING is associate professor of architecture at The Pennsylvania State University. He is director of the Philadelphia Building Workshop, a design-build program for Penn State students in West Philadelphia, Pennsylvania, and codirector of the American Indian Housing Initiative, a community service learning and design-build course providing affordable housing and community buildings for the Northern Cheyenne tribe in Lame Deer, Montana.

Proponents of design-build projects in architectural education often cite the success of teaching technical "how-to" skills to complement or replace standard classroom study and aid students' future professional development. Those opposed to design-build see the act of construction as unnecessary—limited in complexity, inefficient in time spent, needlessly expensive, and presenting risks not worth the rewards. Construction knowledge, it is advised, is better left to technology courses and professional internships.

Debating the merits and inadequacies of design-build projects in teaching construction skills and processes circumscribes one of their central values: that is, design-build provides an educational platform from which architecture is presented as a complex web of ethical positions and actions. As students confront material consequences and physical exhaustion, divergent missions of clients and classmates, and limits of time and money, construction is a vehicle for forging personal definitions of "doing the right thing." So, rather than "teaching" a predetermined code of conduct, design-build creates situations requiring student and faculty to determine ethical conduct and respond.

Experiences in a series of projects at the University of Arkansas led by myself and Eva Kultermann, including the dissection of an early twentieth-century house, the erection of a 140-foot pedestrian bridge, and the making of a prototype Habitat for Humanity house, suggest that design-build projects can extend their value beyond technical issues. In these projects, concerns for personal risk, public safety, and legal liability were weighed against lessons in responsibly reusing resources, improving the quality of the physical and social environment, and honing design skills through the act of making.

A CRASH COURSE IN BUILDING PATHOLOGY

In the first project, first-year students delaminated a 1908 wood-frame house over a three-week period. Here, student safety was of paramount concern, as we preached safe demolition to the students while tetanus shots were delivered.

In this project, the difficult ethical questions centered on the choice between demolition and resuscitation. The house was condemned by the municipality and heading for a bulldozer to landfill death. We realized that by participating in the demolition we were accessories to the crime, only modestly affecting the outcome. We decided that the educational value of participating in the demo, our ability to recycle and reuse material waste, and the public awareness we could amplify through print and television justified our duplicity.

Students escape injury after the porch collapses.

Students stripped the house bare, revealing a glorious white oak frame. We recorded the building's successive additions, deduced the technical weaknesses that led to its decline, and rummaged the remains above and below ground. We cataloged nails and boards, pipes and plaster, and everything in between, reconstituting the house in thirty galvanized steel trashcans in a gallery exhibition. Even though in the end four thirty-yard dumpsters went to the landfill, we did escape without injury and with wood and stone in tow, to be recycled for our next project.

LET US BUILD A BRIDGE

Ethical considerations expanded from student safety to public safety in our design-build project for a pedestrian suspension bridge in the small town of Chester, Arkansas, population ninety. The bridge would connect the town to a public park on the site of three previous bridges washed out by storms over the past one hundred years. We were once again working with first-year students, who were blissfully unaware of how difficult it would be to design and build a bridge of this size in less than four weeks. In the absence of any zoning or building codes in this small town, ethical conduct was squarely upon us. Code-free rural building sites often enable design-build projects to mesh with the educational calendar, yet they test the limits of professional responsibility.

Students researched and designed schemes, first individually and then in groups, before choosing one to build in the remaining two and a half weeks. As Eva and I oversaw some very basic geotechnical and structural issues, students cut wood walkway planks (from the wood frame of the demolished house), assembled cables and hardware fittings, built formwork, and poured concrete. Relative to the norms of professional practice, the speed of our efforts might be seen as irresponsible; yet in teaching, as I balance risks and rewards, I have typically found sufficient value in taking these risks. In turn, young students have shown elevated conduct and performance matching the seriousness of their work.

A concrete bucket brigade forms the anchorages.

Unfortunately, we failed to complete the second anchorage in time and so never gained the full satisfaction of walking the bridge. While we had addressed the possibility of not completing our work with the town's representatives at the outset, the students were disappointed. The bridge was eventually completed, though not to the students' design, by the town. Nonetheless, the people of Chester were deeply grateful, and the students experienced one of the great gifts of design-build public service work: the feeling of genuine appreciation from the people they were assisting.

A HOUSE OF MODEST MEANS

Our design and construction of a Habitat for Humanity house for the Brown family clarifies several ethical issues prompted by construction. Aside from issues of student and public safety and legal liability, we debated the following questions: When is it ethical to reject a client's directive? To what degree should the mission of an architectural education conform to the mission of a nonprofit building partner (Habitat)? What obligations do we have to future inhabitants for adaptation and change? What obligations do we have beyond the site, to the neighborhood and region? What obligations do we have to long-term costs, in durability, energy efficiency, and use of resources?

Fourth- and fifth-year students were asked to design a 1200-square-foot, wheelchair-accessible, four-bedroom house on a 75-by-150-foot south-facing site with a $50,000 construction budget. Complicating matters, the site's slope varied between 5% and 15%, with a storm water–drainage swale carved through the middle of it. During the fall semester students developed designs individually and later in teams, as proposals were shortlisted.

LEFT: Sherman Brown inspects the framing model. RIGHT: The concrete piers and the grade beam lock the foundation into the hillside.

The executive director of Habitat's Fayetteville chapter, in consultation with the Browns, made the final choice of house design. Construction extended for the full spring semester, and the Browns took possession of their house in May 2000.

We identified the issue of long-term costs, not just initial costs, as our ethical imperative for affordable-housing design. To that end, we sought to diminish life-cycle costs through durable building materials and energy-efficient building components and systems. Durability began with the foundation: two-foot-diameter concrete piers, ten feet on center, drilled to resistance and interlocked by a reinforced grade beam. As the foundation perched on unstable weathered shale that had undermined recent Habitat houses (as well as much more expensive houses on the same hillside), we decided on a foundation that would last no matter the cost. Unfortunately, at $10,000 the cost was 20% of our total budget.

The south-facing slope allowed us to easily control solar exposure with overhangs while maximizing daylight. The hillside provided daily microclimate breezes, giving natural ventilation, while a vertical air stack with its rooftop mechanical fan assists air movement in the summer. We beefed up the wood-frame construction from Habitat standards to two-by-six walls, with energy-conserving detailing and cellulose insulation used throughout. We vigorously sealed the building to prevent air infiltration (a blower door test measuring air tightness showed the house was within the top 1% in the state). The efficiency of the shell allowed us to downsize the mechanical system (although we could have done even more if we had known the building would perform so well at the beginning of design). We formed site walls, drainage beds, and walkways using local materials, including stone gathered from the site during construction. Happily, responsible design methods and materials often coincide with having no money for any other option.

Some of our ethical dilemmas were of our own making. Facing tight budget constraints, we frequently debated the merits of designing for safety versus durability. In one quick decision, we chose not to use safety glass in the dormer window, reallocating the three hundred dollars for a waterproof roof underlayment. Here, we directly traded a safety measure for long-term durability. These daily judgments affecting public welfare and pleasure were, for me, a joy as an educator and an all-too-rare alignment of practice and education.

But many of the conflicts we faced during the project were, in part, a result of two communication lapses. First, our design documents were not thorough, leaving many design details unresolved. This was largely intentional, as we encouraged individual student design initiatives to fill in the blanks during the process of building. Unfortunately, Habitat discouraged changes during construction. While we were able to make a few important changes and refinements, the semester-long period for construction restricted our ability to fully consider and present alternatives to our client. We sometimes believed we all would learn more by slowing down, working more deliberately, and debating the merits of varied design approaches, but our ethical decision to ensure the completion of the house drove a construction schedule that conflicted with our ethics of teaching.

The second fundamental communication lapse existed between Habitat and the Brown family. Despite our close contact and friendship with the Browns on the work site, all design decisions were made by Habitat, largely without homeowner involvement. Understandably, Habitat wished to maintain control of their primary mission: providing basic, uniform, affordable shelter to worthy families. We came to understand that our studio's educational mission diverged from Habitat's charge. In our view, Habitat's search for equity had resulted in an architecture irrespective of people and place. And though it was inexpensive and easy to

LEFT: Street view showing the south-facing porch and butterfly dormer. CENTER: Students present the house to the Brown family. RIGHT: The Brown children play in the shade of their front porch.

build, it was not easy to maintain. Our mission sought to design for a specific family organization, tailored to the particularities of site, region, and cultural heritage. In our roles as builders, we had the means to control and implement design in direct response to opportunity and budget constraints. Here, the ethical debate centered on equality versus quality.

As we struggled to respect Habitat's mission and our own, fundamental differences emerged, creating a stream of difficult choices. We battled Habitat's standard "maintenance-free" vinyl siding on the grounds that it was not adaptable to the homeowner's changing tastes in color. Habitat agreed to let us use painted cement board siding with great hesitation, finally recognizing that Mr. Brown's occupation as a house painter made for a unique case.

Our disagreements with Habitat centered around matters considered trivial in most student design projects: a window in a bathroom, a shade of blue paint, transom windows for natural ventilation, an alternative kitchen cabinet layout modestly increasing storage space, a glass panel in the front porch door, and so on. I found these mundane details of design to be the core of our work. As students made impassioned pleas to Habitat's director for the smallest of design issues, I realized the power of design-build to provide an educational platform for the ethical practice of architecture.

On occasion we refused Habitat's directives to change our work. After receiving approvals early for paint colors, we refused to repaint our two-tone color scheme when Habitat notified us that they allowed only one-color houses. More commonly, we attempted to convince Habitat of the wisdom of a design change by building it and showing it to the director. This approach was rarely successful. In one instance, students proposed an alteration in a second floor–bedroom space, increasing usable square footage by removing a wall to a storage room, improving light and room proportions, and avoiding a building code violation. Habitat refused the change, correctly pointing out the new design exceeded their 1200-square-foot space limit. We rebuilt the wall as directed. The decision was devastating to the students, convinced of both the wisdom and "rightness" of their position.

The tense gap between Habitat's and our mission fueled a continuous debate and critique of our role as architects. We were often reminded by Habitat of the danger of custom design if other Habitat families perceived inequities ("design creep," it was termed by Habitat). Students were asked to take responsibility for their work as it affected the wider community and understand Habitat's challenges in negotiating neighborhood suspicions of affordable housing. We, in turn, asked Habitat to consider tailoring their standards for particular site, region, and family circumstances for a qualitatively better living environment, built for longevity and change.

For many, the project was successful. It was on budget, and its systems from foundation to frame are significantly more substantial and it is more energy efficient than typical Habitat projects. It has wonderful light, the students loved making it, and the Browns love living there. But for me, the project failed in its central mission. As architects, we failed to convince an important provider of affordable housing of the benefits of better design. Despite the enthusiasm the project has received, our project is understood as an anomaly, built under special circumstances and not to be repeated. In short, our labor was respected, but not our work. Habitat has continued building houses in the neighborhood: they bear no witness to our efforts.

POSTSCRIPT

University of Arkansas students, under the direction of Eva Kultermann and Greg Herman, completed a second affordable house in spring 2001, although this time not through Habitat. With a similar budget and a less technically challenging site, a local bank financed the house. The homeowners were found and the house sold after all work was complete. In this case, the frustration experienced by the class during construction was a result of the distant involvement of the bank's representatives and uncertainty of the future inhabitants. Here, the students found themselves in the dilemma most architects building affordable housing face: designing for hypothetical clients, thereby making personalized designs difficult. While the detachment eliminated conflict, it also softened the ground under the designer-builder's ethical stands. In hindsight, our conflicts and failures with Habitat had a productive end. They provided a safe haven for the students to construct their own definitions of ethical conduct. This, I believe, is an appropriate activity for future architects and a worthy goal of a university education.

NIRMITHI KENDRA: AN APPROACH TO LOW-COST HOUSING IN INDIA
AMY HAUSE

This examination of housing and construction in a different cultural context—the Nirmithi Kendras of India—can be instructive and perhaps shed light on similar challenges closer to home.

AMY HAUSE teaches and practices architecture in Denver. Her research in India was funded by the Arthur A. and Florence G. Fisher Traveling Scholarship from the Educational Fund of AIA Colorado, awarded to the author in 1997.

A low-cost building program, made up of a constellation of Nirmithi Kendras—community-based building centers that develop and deliver affordable and sustainable construction alternatives—is currently spreading throughout India. In 1996, the United Nations Conference on Human Settlements featured the Nirmithi Kendra (Building Center) as a successful example of a localized solution choreographed by a combination of citizen groups, non-governmental organizations, governments, and the private sector. This approach opposes large-scale, top-down, governmental solutions, which have often resulted in dramatic failures. More fundamentally, the Nirmithi Kendras embody an unusual relationship between government, nongovernmental organizations, and the housing market.

INDIA TODAY

The population of India now exceeds one billion, accounting for 16% of the world's population. The resulting density, 789 people per square mile, compares to stuffing the entire population of the United States into an area a little larger than the state of New Mexico. As a result, India suffers acutely from environmental degradation, mass migrations into its biggest cities, and a shortage of quality affordable housing. In response to these forces, the government of India has sponsored the Nirmithi Kendra program since 1988. Unlike many housing programs, which are based on subsidies to renters and potential homeowners, this network focuses on the research, development, and delivery of low-cost construction systems. The centers emphasize localized organization and skills training to revive depressed village economies, and the use of inexpensive, sustainable design and construction methods that reduce costs and ease environmental burdens.

HISTORIC APPROACHES

India's recent history of housing programs includes a wide range of strategies with varying results. These include centralized government projects such as high-rise apartment buildings and "sites-and-services" developments, as well as approaches that are more community-based.

Groupings of large apartment buildings, essentially densely packed people-storage containers, were a popular housing type in the 1960s and '70s. They were built on cheap plots of leftover land, usually at the periphery of cities. Although currently less favorable than other types of housing projects, they are still being built. These projects often fail because of their placement away from jobs and mass transportation. The design of the high rises also discourages the kind of community interactions that take place in more organically developed Indian village settings. The lack of viable common spaces, or even of particularly useful private outdoor spaces, makes domestic activities such as cooking and overseeing children difficult and isolated from a larger community.

Sites-and-services projects are developments in which the government builds infra-structure—including roads, plumbing, and sometimes toilet structures—and then individual owners, often aided financially, build structures as they need them or have the means to build them. These projects have had mixed results but often run into the same problems as the high-rise projects if located away from jobs and city centers. Though they are not as oblivious to social requirements as the forests of tall apartment buildings tend to be, even the more successful sites-and-services developments are criticized for their overemphasis on physical planning and design, and their inability to recreate venues for social, economic, and religious relationships. Some sites-and-services projects, such as the Aranya Housing

Project designed by architect Balkrishna Doshi in the city of Indore, are more successful because of their thoughtful inclusion of common spaces for community activities and their attention to the human scale.

The more innovative site- and community-specific projects I have investigated include architect Charles Correa's unbuilt proposal for installing water taps at regular intervals on the streets of Mumbai. These water sources were to be used to clean the streets after the vendors had completed their work for the day and before people slept there for the night. Correa designed the width of the sidewalk to be sufficient for both activities. A similar built project in New Delhi involved installing water and sewer infrastructure in a slum area. The typical approach to such a slum would be to ignore or forcibly vacate it. In this case, the addition of water and sewer services improved the living conditions of the inhabitants considerably. Providing actual housing structures was less of a priority here than providing infrastructure, because the inhabitants could relatively easily find basic building materials and create shelters on their own.

While I was traveling in India visiting various housing projects, I experienced a personal lesson in the importance of involving the end users in the design process and the difficulty, as a designer, of anticipating their needs. I visited a housing project designed by Kamu Iyer, Architects, for steel mill workers and their families in the town of Vysankere, in the state of Karnataka. The houses were attractively designed and were made of beautiful, locally quarried granite blocks. I was invited into the home of a couple with three children—a two-room house with an enclosed outdoor space leading to small shower and toilet area. One of the two rooms contained the kitchen, where I noticed built into the floor a solid granite mortar for grinding spices. I made special note of the sensitivity of this design detail, considering the importance of spices in Indian cuisine. The couple then took me to their other room, where they showed me their two most prized possessions, a television and the food processor that they actually use to grind spices.

THE NIRMITHI KENDRA PROGRAM

In general, projects that offer more opportunities for input by the end user and participation by the community have succeeded to a greater degree than those developed by government agencies without much community involvement. The Indian government has taken these results seriously and responded with programs, including some of the approaches listed above, that are more sensitive to their clients. It is in this spirit that, in 1986, the Nirmithi Kendra program was developed.

The system of Nirmithi Kendras (also referred to as just "Kendras") is based on the idea that construction costs are high, increasing faster than the rate of inflation. A reduction in these costs means that a greater proportion of the population will be able to afford housing. The program, then, is centered around a handful of research and development (R&D) organizations that are developing building technologies and materials that are more affordable and sustainable than conventional ones. These organizations include private research institutes, universities, and nongovernmental organizations (NGOs). The role of the network of Kendras, which includes more than five hundred Kendras spread throughout the country, is to transfer this technology from these laboratories to the construction field for widespread application. The system accomplishes this by supplying the market with materials, construction methods, and services that a broader sector of the population can access and afford to purchase. Clients and customers range from government agencies that wish to have large-scale low-income housing projects designed and built, to individuals purchasing small amounts of building materials.

ORGANIZATION

The network of Kendras is sponsored by the government of India through federal, state, and local grants and coordinated by the Housing and Urban Development Corporation. HUDCO has published a booklet that defines how to set up a Kendra, explaining everything from where to find grants, to the recommended management structure of the individual center, to how to obtain land, to what activities might take place at the center. HUDCO's policy for the Kendras emphasizes flexibility: "Organizational forms of building centers should be flexible, in favor of an entrepreneurial, non-bureaucratic set-up that ensures operational autonomy."[1] Each Kendra is required to have a governing body or executive committee that includes representatives from the government, HUDCO, and an approved R&D organization. This body is responsible for the overall direction of the Kendra.

[1] **Housing and Urban Development Corporation, Ltd. (HUDCO),** *National Network of Building Centers Action Plan Manual* **(HUDCO: n.p., 1995), 2.**

Kendras have been started by NGOs, educational institutions, construction worker cooperatives, and entrepreneurs; many of them become self-sustaining. The variety of management structures has resulted in the Kendras offering combinations of R&D design, construction, consulting, manufacturing (of materials), and training (of skilled laborers). For example, one research institution may focus on the refinement of compressed stabilized mud block and other appropriate construction, while another entrepreneurial center may focus on the manufacturing and distribution of these materials, and still a third, perhaps a government-run center, may focus on training laborers to build with these materials and technologies. Often Kendras include all of the above.

One example of a successful Kendra is the Nirmithi National Institute of Habitat Management, which was set up specifically to train architects and engineers to manage other Kendras. Another is the National Institute of Construction and Research, which offers training in construction using specific Kendra technologies developed by other R&D centers. Its mission has been to identify problems of construction workers, evolve training and certificate programs for various trade skills, and publish manuals related to the program's alternative technologies. These two Kendras illustrate how the program is not driven by any one particular component, but rather attempts to include the full range of the construction industry, from architects to workers.

SOCIAL AND ECONOMIC CONTEXT

The Nirmithi Kendra system relies on democratic organizational structures and market-friendly small business possibilities that run against deeply ingrained Indian traditions. The government of India and HUDCO actively encourage entrepreneurs to set up for-profit Kendras "for penetrating the building center program into the larger segments of the housing delivery market."[2] Professor K. S. Jagadish of the Center for Application of Science and Technology to Rural Areas (ASTRA), one of the network's primary research laboratories, described his frustration with the lack of entrepreneurial spirit in India,

Building crew from ASTRA.

[2] **Ibid.**

which, he feels, makes the transfer of knowledge from laboratory to the construction industry slow and difficult. He believes that one of the sources of this problem is that much of the population desires the job security of a government post, since India's history of cumbersome regulation has inhibited risk-taking in the private sector. I think another problem is that an entrepreneurial instinct is in opposition to India's caste system, which defines a narrow range of work possibilities a person is expected to follow.

The Kendras must be sensitive to how their work is perceived by the general population with regard to caste and class. Many people with whom I spoke at the Kendras went out of their way to make a distinction between low-income housing and low-cost construction. They emphasized that what they do is the latter, because it is appropriate for everyone and for all building types. Low-income housing, on the other hand, implies a specific building type and specific target population. The Kendras wish to popularize these construction materials and methods among all economic groups to avoid stigmatizing them as "low-caste." To do so, they embrace clients from all economic sectors. Their work includes both higher-end single-family residences and lower-end institutional work; this allows for a greater exploration of mixing the innovative, traditional, and indigenous construction typical of Nirmithi Kendra architecture. This research has broadened the aesthetic possibilities of the materials and methods, and has also helped to establish a favorable reputation for this type of construction.

The mission of the Nirmithi Kendra program includes progressive ideas about the empowerment of women. Despite the narrow gender roles to which women are often assigned in India, the Kendras take an active approach to the inclusion of women in professional and leadership roles by training them to be skilled laborers. These skills, traditionally held by men, offer many women considerable economic independence that would otherwise be difficult for them to achieve in Indian culture. Women also hold prominent leadership and management roles in the network of Kendras.

Water tower under construction in the community of Auroville in the state of Tamil Nadu, southern India.

DESIGN

The Kendras' nonhierarchical organizational structure and their emphasis on materials have an effect on building design. Although they (deliberately) do not define what constitutes good design, the underlying philosophies of the program point in specific directions.

The focus on environmental sustainability and local materials leads to a design process in sympathy with nature and the local climate. The desire to make the materials available to a large sector of the population has resulted in low-tech materials that many people will have the skills to work with. These factors result in a design bias toward indigenous building types, and, not surprisingly, the Kendras have researched and often promoted regional indigenous construction methods and building types or have reinterpreted them for contemporary use.

The emphasis on low-tech materials and community-based design also inhibits the unfortunate high rises previously discussed. Although I saw some lovely institutional buildings that various Kendras designed, the tallest was about five stories.

A compressed stabilized mud block house under construction at ASTRA in Bangalore, Karnataka.

The Kendras offer more specific design direction at the detail level. They carefully research, publish, and disseminate the use of traditional and newly developed materials and methods, then issue books that illustrate, often in pictures only, how to appropriately build with this palette of materials.

MATERIALS AND TECHNOLOGIES

Because the relative costs of labor to materials is low in India compared to the United States, the technologies promoted by the Nirmithi Kendra network often seem, by U.S. standards, to be labor-intensive ones that result in only small savings of raw materials. However, these technologies show cost savings of 20–40% compared to conventional construction.

The materials and technologies are generally low-tech ones that take advantage of local resources and environmental factors, and tend to correspond with the principles of environmental sustainability. Local resources are generally preferred to imported or transported alternatives because of the added fuel and labor costs involved in shipping. Low-tech materials, such as mud and clay, are generally preferred to energy-intensive, processed materials, such as steel and concrete. Since energy is also an expensive resource, long-term energy-efficient technologies such as bio-gas, wind, and solar energy are also promoted by the Kendras. Jagadish emphasized the importance of popularizing sustainability as an ethical standard within the building industry and the broader culture. He observed that Indians have the tendency to want to consume resources "just like Americans do," when given the opportunity.

Other alternative materials promoted by the Kendras include compressed stabilized mud blocks, which are building blocks made of soil and a stabilizing agent such as portland cement, and terra cotta tiles, which are baked earth tiles that can be used for roofing, flooring, and infill panels in concrete. Materials specific to particular regions also play a prominent role in the Nirmithi Kendra construction. In the state of Kerala, where coconut palms are abundant, coconut shells are used as infill pieces in concrete, coconut fiber is used for carpeting, and coconut wood is used for window and doorframes.

The Kolaghat Building Center in the state of West Bengal focuses on the production of fly ash clay bricks. Standard clay bricks require clay that is also fertile agricultural soil and are produced using fossil fuels (timber and coal). The technology for the fly ash clay bricks save on both soil and fuel.

It is not surprising that local materials and regional architectural styles emerge in this community-based program. Environmental considerations, material costs, and the emphasis on local self-reliance all point to this solution and enable communities to make use of local resources and respond to specific problems and needs.

THE NIRMITHI KENDRA NETWORK AS A MODEL

In 1993, the United Nations Commission on Human Settlements recommended that the Nirmithi Kendra network be a model for programs in other developing countries. It was also included on the UN's Best Practices list in 1996.

Although the program clearly has much to offer, it should not be understood as a comprehensive solution to the housing shortage in India or anywhere else. While it can place housing within the reach of a larger percentage of India's population through the reduction of construction costs, it will clearly never directly address the portion of the population with the greatest needs.

The program's potential success in other countries comes from its flexible structure and the fact that it is designed to adapt to local conditions and resources. This flexibility allows the Kendras to act as laboratories where effective relationships between communities, nonprofits, government, the market, and the environment can be tested and analyzed. This structure enables constant and direct feedback, and therefore a continuous evolution of the program itself.

RED FEATHER DEVELOPMENT GROUP

ROBERT YOUNG, INTERVIEWED BY JEFF EVANS

The following narrative tracks the development of a cause, from one man reading a newspaper article about a local Native-American tribe, to his developing a close relationship with a member of the community, to the construction of her house, and on to a program that has finished thirty-three house-based projects.

ROBERT YOUNG founded the Red Feather Development group in 1994 and currently serves as executive director. He has overseen the successful completion of over thirty-three housing-based projects. For more information about Red Feather, please visit their Website at www.redfeather.org.

JEFF EVANS graduated from the University of Virginia in 2000 and served as a Design Corps Fellow for two years following graduation. As a fellow, his contributions included serving as the chair for the Structures for Inclusion 2 conference, and working with RBGC on Bayview and First Baptist Church.

One morning back in 1992, while eating breakfast at a cafe in Taos, New Mexico, I came across an article in a local newspaper about elderly American tribal members freezing to death on the reservations. This stuck with me, and I wanted to find out more. But I was unable to because it was not reported by any other news organization. This also stuck with me. Tragic situations around the globe draw media attention and call people to help with them. Why then was this tragedy that was so close to home being overlooked?

I decided to get firsthand information about what it was like to live on the reservations. I found out about an adopt-a-grandparent program, in which people are paired with a Lakota elder. I liked this program because it meant more than just giving money; it offered the chance to get to know a person. I was paired with Katherine Red Feather, who was seventy-seven years old and lived on the Pine Ridge reservation in South Dakota, in what has been the poorest county in the United States for the past fifteen years. Katherine and I started writing letters and sharing our life stories. It was eye opening to learn about what was going on in her life. She had no running water and no electricity. These are supposedly Third World conditions, but they were here in the United States.

One year after we began to write letters, I visited Pine Ridge. Katherine is tough, so she was definitely surviving, but she lived in the worst situation I had ever seen. She was occupying a car trailer and the shell of a school bus. As you can imagine, her home was incredibly hot in the summer and very cold in the winter. This was the norm on the reservation, not the exception.

I left the reservation thinking there had to be others working to alleviate these conditions and wanting to join them to do this type of work. So I began to do research. I found there were two types of organizations working for reservations: religious groups and the federal government. The religious-based programs offered Band-Aids at best and had strings attached to their assistance. The federal programs were woefully inadequate. Neither appealed to me as a way in which I could help and make a difference.

After talking over this dilemma with some friends, we all decided to build Katherine a home. I raised funds for one year for this project and filed for 501(c)(3) nonprofit status for our group.

So we built Katherine a home. It was a typical stick-frame kit home provided for us by Miles Homes, a manufacturer that heard about our work. Many groups of people helped us with this first home. Miles Homes sent people to help us build it. Friends of mine who were builders helped. Katherine's family helped also. It took us two weeks to build the home. It was difficult. While we were there, we really bonded with the local community. This affected me; I could really see myself doing more of this type of work.

Since I had cofounded a private label clothing company, I knew about business. I then read *Revolution of the Heart* by Bill Shore, a book that discussed how a nonprofit could be run like a successful business. I knew that, if I wanted to, I could undertake the work we had just begun as a full-time mission. That was how Red Feather Development Group was founded.

Red Feather has a two-prong mission: to educate the public about the plight of tribal members on reservations throughout the West, with a focus on the Northern Plains; and to put that education into action by building homes and teaching aspects of home construction to tribal members so they can be self-sufficient. To have a real impact on communities, work must be done with them and not to them.

At Red Feather, we wanted to come up with a home-building program and be involved with home rehabilitation. A federal program called Indian Health Services brings water and electricity to homes that are up to code, but the families on reservations could not afford the necessary renovations. So Red Feather brings homes up to code. We saw the impact that having a home could have on a family. It went from just surviving to not having to worry about survival.

Strawbale construction of "Martha's House" under way in Northern Cheyenne Reservation, Montana.

We knew that we wanted, in addition to fixing homes, to build homes for families. Our project ideas come from both the outside and inside the group. Some people track us down, but we also find some homes for rehabilitation. We decided to build strawbale homes because stick-frame construction is a waste of trees. On the Great Plains, there is no wood but tons of wheat and straw. Other groups had recommended strawbale homes to the tribes, but no one had researched their use. We did not know how long they would last or how to best utilize them for structures.

One day, a volunteer of ours, by chance, saw some strawbale work that students at the University of Washington had completed. Red Feather soon formed a partnership with the departments of construction management and architecture at the University of Washington and decided to build a strawbale home together as an experiment. Red Feather raised money for the home, architecture students designed it, and construction management faculty and students provided the technical expertise. Both faculty and students came to South Dakota and helped us build the home. In the future, students will participate through a for-credit seminar.

In our first project together, the students were taking a leadership role and were directing more experienced volunteers. That is not what is best for them or for Red Feather. We recently hired our own construction coordinator, who has a background in architecture. The students work with him and other experienced volunteers to interpret their designs into buildings.

We have finished thirty-three housing-based projects. These projects include rehabilitations, renovations, and additions as simple as a handicap ramp. We have finished two strawbale homes, one at Pine Ridge and one at the Crow reservation in south central Montana. The two are completely different designs, because the students wanted to improve the design based on what they learned from building the first home. The tribes wanted hands-on knowledge, so they joined in the construction. This was not common for reservations, because peo-

Client and construction team in front of the finished house.

ple who live on them are often too worried about daily survival to consider volunteering. Together we put the walls up in six hours. People started to show up and say, "Wow."

For the first two homes, the recipient families had very little say in the design. It was an experiment for them, as well. For future homes, we envision a standard kitchen and main bath core that is built outside the home. We could even use the manufacturing of these core units to create jobs. (Many tribes rely on casinos for employment, but only a handful are successful. There is also great casino competition from the private sector, so tribes need to diversify and get other businesses going and then reinvest.) Then, the walls would be built with the community) and family. We recognize that families differ, one home will not appeal to all of them. The U.S. Department of Housing and Urban Development tried the one-size-fits-all method on the reservations, and it did not work.

Red Feather is driven by the many volunteers who help on a day-to-day basis. We had only two paid employees for a long time. We have an involved board of six, as well as ten advisers. Volunteers, along with the community members, build the homes. During the building sessions, volunteers pay a fee that covers their food and camp facilities. The conditions during our projects are extreme, ranging from very hot to very cold. Yet, on our last Pine Ridge project, we had to turn down 260 potential volunteers. We purposefully keep Red Feather small believing in walking before you run. Right now, we are focusing on the homeowners and not on the volunteers. Our list of volunteers keeps growing, though, and is up to over 700 people. We also have over 4,000 people on our mailing list.

We have focused since the beginning on developing our own self-sufficiency. We had little choice, as most foundations will not fund groups unless they are established three to five years. We have had great support from the band Pearl Jam, which did a benefit concert for us. Robert Redford profiled us in the Sundance catalog and allowed his customers to add money to their orders to be donated to Red Feather. We work at marketing our projects and getting in the media. We put together a film, and I am going to travel and talk to corporations and tribal members in fund-raising efforts.

Living room of Martha's House with son's taxidermy on the walls.

We try to get unrestricted funds that are not project specific. We are in unknown territory, so we need to stay adaptable. We have a good record of achievement in the reservations compared to the constant failure by the federal government. Foundations are more supportive of us now, but individuals provide our main support.

Red Feather does not take money from the federal government. Think about the long relationship between the U.S. government and the tribal members. Historical actions have caused tribal members to distrust the government. Red Feather wants to bridge the gap between the reservations and the rest of the country; we want tribal members to trust us. Therefore, we do not take any money with strings attached.

Red Feather has had tribal member support. Understand that there are well over 300 distinct tribal cultures or nations. When we undertook a project on the Crow Reservation and the Northern Cheyenne came over to help. Their historical grudges go back a thousand years. It was great to see the tribes work together. They understand that they can accomplish more by joining forces. Red Feather does not have particularly strong ties to any specific tribes. We want to work in the worst areas with the most need first, and so are concentrating our efforts on the Northern Plains. We work on the Pine Ridge Reservation and Rosebud Reservation in South Dakota, and the Crow Reservation and the Northern Cheyenne Reservation in south central Montana.

Red Feather seeks to build homes in a sustainable fashion, not only in the environmental sense, but also in the sense that our homes are sustained by the community. We have not yet looked into incorporating other elements of sustainable design, like harvesting passive solar energy or capturing rainwater. There are on average three hundred days of sunshine a year in the Northern Plains, so passive or active solar systems can easily equal savings on energy bills. The double-back walls are also energy efficient. With the savings on their mortgages (which owners take out for some of the materials and labor for their homes), they can spend money locally and keep the dollars on the reservation. In the long run, we at Red Feather want to run clinics to teach sustainable-building techniques. We are working with tribal colleges to teach sustainable building to carpenters. We want the University of Washington to use its expertise in teaching to put together manuals about building and materials.

We would like to have a community-development corporation on each reservation managed by each tribe. We are an outside organization and not tribal members—we want to put this project into their hands. We encourage self-sufficiency. Until the program is managed by each tribe, it will not mean as much to them. We want an office on each reservation that would work to provide technical advice and research. The families would then determine what they want to build. Graduate students could go out for a summer to work on home design to make the process more efficient. The community development offices will give the reservations more power to control their own futures.

Katherine Red Feather is doing just fine in her new home, the home that originally inspired the Red Feather Development Group. Despite having very little money, her family is keeping up the house and has added a few plants to the front of it. I believe Katherine's new home has had a hugely positive impact on her life, and hope that future Red Feather projects might do the same for others.

3 / BUILDING WITH A COMMUNITY

REBUILDING BAYVIEW: COMMUNITY DESIGN AS A CATALYST FOR SOCIAL CHANGE

MAURICE D. COX

This investigation explores how the community of Bayview on the Eastern Shore of Virginia used a participatory design process as a community consensus builder and catalyst for physical and social change. Through neighborhood meetings, community events, and design workshops, they successfully charted a long-term plan to rebuild their community as a new rural village, while addressing some of their most pressing environmental needs.

MAURICE D. COX is an architectural educator, urban designer, and Mayor of the City of Charlottesville, Virginia. He is associate professor of architecture at the University of Virginia and a partner in the firm RBGC Architecture.Research.Urbanism, founded in 1996.

Rebuilding a community begins with the ability of ordinary citizens to influence the important planning decisions that affect their lives. When citizens are poor, black, and living in debilitating physical and environmental conditions, desires to exercise such basic rights can become an insurmountable battle for social equity and environmental justice. To overcome these obstacles, the community of Bayview, Virginia, built a nontraditional coalition comprised of a local environmental conservationist, civil rights activists, and an interdisciplinary team of design experts. The group envisioned a village of collectively owned affordable homes without stigma, neighborhood-owned businesses, community institutions, and public places, all set in a productive agricultural landscape.

The existing state of the substandard rental housing created conditions beyond repair.

THE SITUATION

The Eastern Shore of Virginia is physically isolated from the rest of Virginia by the Chesapeake Bay and a ten-mile bridge/tunnel. The result is an economical and psychological separation that has kept the peninsula one of the best-preserved ecosystems on the East Coast but also one of the poorest regions of Virginia. The small community of Bayview dates back to the time of the Emancipation, and many of its fifty-two families can trace their roots back 350 years, to the earliest days of slavery on Virginia's Eastern Shore. Bayview residents today remain among Northampton County's poorest citizens living in rural isolation and substandard living conditions. Most families reside in rented two-room shacks with no indoor plumbing or bathrooms. Outhouses, 95% percent of which are not functioning or are in desperate need of repair, litter their backyards. The only water supply for the majority of families is pumped by hand from three outdoor pitcher pumps connected to wells too shallow to reach sanitary water.

This extraordinarily fragile community was the proposed site of a maximum-security prison in 1994, making it the most contested ground in the region and the center of a three-year battle. Bayview Citizens for Social Justice, a grassroots organization founded by two African-American women of Bayview, Alice Coles and Cozzie Lockwood, led the effort to stop its construction. Their struggle to defeat the prison proposal was a clear act of self-preservation. Residents of Bayview realized that their mission to improve their quality of life was really an issue of environmental justice. Their decision to continue their journey of self-determination with the Nature Conservancy, a large and influential land conservation organization, was a statement of political defiance. The Nature Conservancy was aware that the success of its campaign depended on expanding the environmental agenda to

Alice Coles stands as a symbol of defiance in front of Coles Chapel.

include human, social, and economic equity for the poor. The two groups pledged to work in a partnership of mutual trust to eliminate the substandard living conditions of Bayview. In 1997, their partnership resulted in the award of a $20,000 Environmental Justice Grant

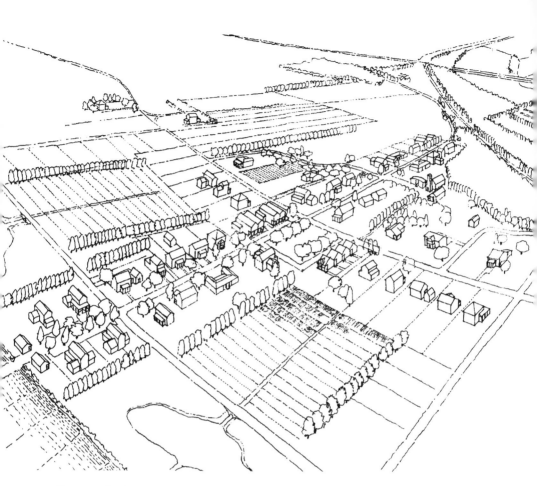

The community plan proposes a system of three streets that extend from the tracts of the existing village and terminate in community-owned agricultural fields.

from the Environmental Protection Agency (EPA) to create a year-long process leading to a community-based action plan.

THE MISSION

The stated mission of the Environmental Justice Grant was to "identify and solve pollution problems resulting from substandard drinking water, waste water, and storm water conditions in the economically and socially stressed African-American neighborhood of Bayview." To meet this goal, the leadership of Bayview, with the assistance of the Nature Conservancy, assembled an interdisciplinary team of experts from across the state. My architectural office, RBGC, and I acted as lead facilitators in collaboration with an environmental engineer from Old Dominion University, an environmental planner, and the Nature Conservancy, acting as fiscal agent. The technical design team quickly expanded to include representatives from the

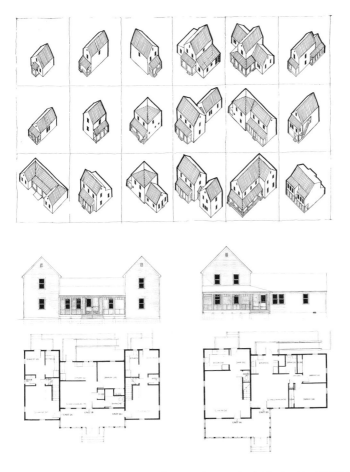

TOP: Sketches of possible variations of house designs meet a variety of residents' needs.
ABOVE: Two housing types interpret the Eastern Shore farm vernacular through a series
of aggregate massings that provide for a variety of family compositions.

local National Association for the Advancement of Colored People (NAACP) and the Citizens
for a Better Eastern Shore.

They learned from their very first encounter with the citizens of Bayview that the
entire community was determined to change their physical reality. The technical team
was challenged to elevate the design process so that it became an opportunity for community empowerment; this would shift radically the balance of power from a county
bureaucracy to a community of low-income residents. The process would not simply provide short- and long-term solutions to significant environmental issues, but would create
a community-based organization able to implement them. The technical team believed
that by interpreting the community's vision of itself, instigating an organizational structure, and setting Bayview on a political path of self-governance, a defined community
identity would emerge.

THE PROCESS

The planning process unfolded over the course of one year and consisted of ten encounters between the technical team and the Bayview community. Workshops were organized as community events to gather oral history, assess existing environmental and housing conditions, share resulting information, identify short-term actions, and introduce alternative concepts for the community's future plan. The format of the workshops adapted to Bayview's customary forms of social gathering, in which residents traditionally congregate for worship and celebration. The first event involved residents simply coming together to tell the collective story of their community. Another took the form of a neighborhood clean-up juxtaposed to an exhibition of photographs documenting the physical decay of their homes. A fish fry fund-raiser was combined with the design team's presentation of rural village development alternatives. The inauguration of new wells and final unveiling of the Bayview rural village plan were celebrated with a gospel concert jubilee of choirs coming to wish Bayview residents well. These were but a few of the mechanisms used to give the process a celebratory quality and broaden community attendance.

Storytelling proved to be among the most effective tool for gathering information about the collective history of the community. The goal was to inspire residents to envision Bayview as it once was and to incorporate that spirit in any formal structure proposed for a new community. An old roadside potato barn and a one-room chapel engulfed in the brush still stood as fragmentary reminders of their collective history. Despite their current substandard living conditions, residents were able to recall a prouder, more prosperous time when Bayview was a productive village of farmers. Family stories about working the land helped to expand the physical boundaries of the study area to include the surrounding fields.

While envisioning a formal structure for their future community, Bayview residents were encouraged to establish short-term goals that could be accomplished within the planning year. Their goals were to take inventory of Bayview's current environmental and housing conditions, drill a series of new deep wells for safe drinking water, demolish vacant substandard housing wherever possible, replace all nonfunctioning pit-privies, and rid their community of years of uncollected trash. The strategy was to set goals that could be incrementally achieved by the community. With each accomplishment residents strengthened both their organizational skills and their confidence in the ability to achieve a better future.

THE OUTCOME

The spiritual rebirth of this community and the present-day political process of community empowerment is still underway in Bayview. Ten months after the beginning of the community-planning process, Bayview Citizens for Social Justice became incorporated as a first step toward becoming a nonprofit tax-exempt corporation. They had realized all short-term goals they set out to achieve, from drilling deep wells, to providing clean drinking water, to planting a community garden, to rekindling belief in a productive agricultural landscape. Citizens unanimously endorsed a long-term vision of their community rebuilt as a rural village of homes, neighborhood-owned business, community institutions, and collectively owned land. By securing an option to purchase forty-three acres of adjacent agricultural land, BCSJ showed how they could take tangible steps to develop, own, and operate their village.

TOP: The Bayview community center is an interpretation of a popular Eastern Shore vernacular type: the big house, little house, colonnade, and kitchen. ABOVE: The assembly hall references traditional spiritual gatherings and provides for the community their only option to congregate indoors.

The barn serves as a marketplace for the community to sell the produce from their agricultural cooperative.

This extraordinary experience has once more confirmed the importance of the designer's role in enabling communities to achieve social change by providing tools to help them shape and control their own destiny. In building and defining their future, the community of Bayview demonstrated how seemingly powerless people, acting collectively, can become very powerful.

ACTIVIST PRACTICE: THE RISKY BUSINESS OF DEMOCRATIC DESIGN

ROBERTA M. FELDMAN

Universities are in a unique position to support access to and effective use of design knowledge. The University of Illinois at Chicago's City Design Center merges design education with social activism.

ROBERTA M. FELDMAN is an architectural educator and researcher who is codirector of the City Design Center, College of Architecture and the Arts, the University of Illinois at Chicago, a cross-disciplinary design research and outreach program that promotes the study and practice of design in the public interest. Her book, *The Dignity of Resistance: Women Residents' Activism in Public Housing*, coauthored with Susan Stall, will be published in 2003 by Cambridge University Press.

It is fashionable today, as it has been in the past, to dismiss design's contribution to social justice. Work merging activism and design remains marginalized within the profession of architecture. Professional and educational institutions all too often support the economically and politically powerful in our society, and the cultural elite. As Robert Gutman has aptly noted, these institutions are the "soft cops," enforcing the power elite's agenda through design.

While standard professional services are both vital and necessary for all members of society, I believe they are not sufficient. Design as an activist profession can work to restructure the relationships between those who make community design decisions and those who are affected by these decisions. We must consider these two questions: Who has access to design information? Who has a say in architectural decision-making? In the United States, design decisions are made by a small minority of people. If the goal of activist practice is social justice, then these decisions must include people who have traditionally had minimal say. But decision-making power alone is not enough. The capabilities to make effective, informed design decisions also are necessary.

Universities are in a unique position to support access to and effective use of design knowledge. At the City Design Center of the University of Illinois at Chicago (UIC), we are merging design education with social activism. This mission is not without precedent. There is a long history of university-based community design centers as well as individual architecture faculty using their design skills in support of social justice.

At the City Design Center, we have taken on the challenge to support informed community design decisions as central to our mission. Over the past eight years, the City Design Center has worked with over thirty nonprofit organizations on over fifty projects based in low-income communities. Our projects range in scale from as large as a town, to neighborhood centers and corridors, to buildings, to as small as streetscape elements.

To accomplish our goals, we work in cross-professional and disciplinary collaborations. We believe that effective activist design practice cannot be accomplished by architects acting alone. The City Design Center brings together UIC faculty and students in architecture, planning, environmental graphic design, public and community art, history and culture of cities, and other related disciplines to work collaboratively on projects. And we develop partnerships between UIC faculty and students, design professionals, community groups and institutions, and governmental agencies to work on design issues of mutual concern in the Chicago region.

Students participate in all our community design work and, in the process, broaden their education to make the linkages among theory, practice, and social interests. We teach them how to communicate and share design knowledge with a broad audience, not just their peers. Working with communities underserved by the design professions introduces students to alternative, democratic design practices and encourages civic responsibility. But even more importantly, we do not shield the students from the contested terrain of real-world projects. In addition to working collaboratively across design disciplines, students work with community leaders, public officials, and others who have the power to inform and implement their projects. We ask the students, with the faculty's advice, to deal with the economic and political problems that arise during their work. In other words, we let the problems get messy.

There are tradeoffs, however, between these educational benefits for students and the expertise needed to execute a community design project. We inform our community partners of the students' limited experience, their educational requirements, and the necessary time commitment for student interaction. Our partners request these services accepting these limitations because the services are free or at a very low cost. And often the community partners gain unexpected benefits from the wide range of students' schemes, especially alternative approaches to those the partners had considered.

OUR COMMUNITY DESIGN METHODS

Given our mission—design in the service of social justice—it is not surprising that we rely on participatory design processes to engage our community clients in environmental design decision-making. The participatory design methods we use are rooted in the conviction that both our clients and we—as architects, planners, graphic designers, and other design professionals—have the necessary expertise to guide effective and socially just design decisions. To support informed design decision-making, we engage in an educational process that is based on mutual respect and understanding of one another's expertise. Our clients have the most and best knowledge about their own situations—the problems with their current circumstances, and their future needs and desires. We have knowledge about alternative design solutions, many of which may be unfamiliar to our client.

We create contexts in which this knowledge can be shared and informed design decisions made using one or more of the following methods. We engage the community in identifying their needs and aspirations. We research, document, and communicate design knowledge, for instance, about relevant functional and innovative design ideas and practices, and share this information with the community in a form they can readily understand. We create a range of relevant, alternative design strategies to support choice. We engage the community in a dialogue about the costs and benefits of the alternative design strategies. In all the methods, we restrain from imposing our desires on the community's ultimate design decisions.

While these methods can result in empowering communities to make their own informed design decisions, this desired result is not guaranteed. Activist practice is a risky business. In particular, we have found that as soon as we attempt to democratize knowledge, we politicize knowledge. Dare I use the cliché: knowledge is power, and this power is not always easily shared. These difficulties are best described by example.

INTERNET-BASED DESIGN AND DEVELOPMENT INFORMATION SYSTEMS

One of the means the City Design Center has used to disseminate state-of-the-art design knowledge and hard-to-get information to the general public is the Internet. In particular, we maintain two Websites: the Chicago Imagebase, a catalog of the Chicago region's historic and contemporary built environment, and Design Matters, which documents best practices in affordable housing nationwide.

The development of these Websites went smoothly until we began to include information, in particular on the Imagebase, that could be used for political or economic advantage. Four Community Development Corporations located in one Chicago neighborhood were interested in creating with us an Internet-based property monitoring system for use in their community revitalization plans. This system would keep track of all information necessary for property development, including existing land use, condition of building structures, ownership, real-estate tax status, and others. While each nonprofit corporation had the same objective, initially each wanted a proprietary system. Each Community Development Corporation had their own development objectives, some of which might compete with the other organizations. More critically, the Community Development Corporations were concerned about the information falling into the hands of private developers. (The eastern boundary of the neighborhood where they were working was under the threat of gentrification.) As a public university, however, UIC is committed to providing public information. It took considerable time for us to facilitate an accord between these nonprofit organizations to collaborate on the project, as well as to gain an agreement to keep the information available to the general public.

We developed the Design Matters Internet catalog to identify exemplary affordable housing design projects nationwide and to share this information with housing producers, policymakers, and "consumers"—that is, the future residents of affordable housing developments.

During construction of the Design Matters site, we collected nearly three hundred projects through nominations and an open call. A City Design Center project team and an advisory committee of affordable housing experts selected projects based on construction and life-cycle costs, aesthetic quality, household and community fit, adaptability, universal accessibility, energy and resource efficiency, healthy indoor environments, and safety and security. Approximately seventy-five projects in the United States are documented in the catalog.

Chicago Mayor Richard M. Daley dedicating the Brown School play lot, designed by Philip Enquist and Toni Griffin of Skidmore Owings and Merrill, with assistance from the UIC City Design Center.

Over the past two years since the catalog was launched, we have been informed that it is being used to meet some of our objectives. Numerous Community Development Corporations across the nation have accessed the site and used the information to improve the designs of their housing developments; affordable housing proponents have used the cited projects in their efforts to combat resistance to affordable housing in their communities; a state government's affordable-housing committee has used the design objectives in their recommendations for future housing policies; and architects in the field of affordable housing have praised our effects to make a case for the importance of design in affordable-housing production. Yet these are all the anticipated parties involved in producing affordable housing. We have no way to assess if this information has reached the ultimate users, the future residents of these developments, putting the information into the hands of those most affected by affordable-housing design decisions. Nor does the availability of this information to these users assure that they will have an appropriate role to play in the design of their homes.

In developing the catalog, we emphasized particular design objectives, those that are considered particularly relevant to affordable-housing excellence in the United States. These criteria, however, are not necessarily transferable to other cultural contexts, and their imposition certainly would not serve social justice. For instance, we have begun to develop collaborations with academic institutions in Canada and Mexico to expand the catalog coverage. Our colleagues in Universal Autonoma Metropolitana in Mexico City, however, were reticent at first, primarily because of the particular design objectives we were emphasizing. Not surprisingly, the affordable-housing development and design community in Mexico does not have all the same priorities. For instance, environmental sustainability was viewed as a difficult, if not inappropriate, goal for a Third World country. Universal design also had not yet become a priority. It was agreed that each country's catalogers would identify and address those design objectives that are particularly relevant to their context.

DEVELOPMENT SCENARIOS FOR A SMALL TOWN

To contest the status quo, community design centers work to support organizations and individuals that are outside of the power elite. We were asked by a working-class, small town in Illinois to assist in engaging the community in a dialog about their future growth. This town was experiencing development pressures because of a new highway only miles from its center. In particular, the mayor requested alternative plans that would accommodate the town's growth and the town center's redevelopment, while meeting the needs and interests of all the community residents. As part of an ongoing collaborative UIC architecture and planning graduate design studio, the CityLab, faculty and students created development scenarios to serve as a basis for discussion. A community forum was held with all of the town's stakeholders, and four development models were chosen for elaboration.

When the draft of the final report was presented to the mayor, he told us not to distribute it to the forum participants. Needless to say, the faculty and students who had worked on the project were stunned. When they asked "Why?," we were given no explanation. Subsequently, we found out that a powerful stakeholder and financial supporter of the mayor had favored only one of the development models and wanted only that model presented. A political battled ensued. Relying on our contract and our commitment to all the community members who had participated, we refused to give in. Ultimately, because of political pressure on the university, we were obliged not to distribute the report.

THE BENEFITS OF THE COMMUNITY DEVELOPMENT CORPORATION

Political tensions are not the only types of risks that university-based community design centers face. Faculty workloads are taxed, and the rewards—including monetary rewards, professional recognition, and academic advancement—are tenuous. Centers like ours, which are multidisciplinary, also face the challenge of integrating the different theories and practices of planning, architecture, and related fields. And because we rely heavily on student work, the quality of the designs and plans produced for the community may be uneven. The community may not be served as well as if professionals had completed the projects. So why do we do it?

All I can answer is: It is the right thing to do. As a public institution in the heart of a major city in the United States, I believe UIC has the responsibility and capacity to utilize its resources to provide useful information in the service of community-building and neighborhood revitalization, while at the same time offering students a design education that both broadens their expertise and supports social justice.

THE DREAMTREE PROJECT: FORGING COMMUNITY RELATIONSHIPS
MARK S. GOLDMAN

Inclusive decision making in a community project can be a complex challenge for the designer who seeks consensus. Artists, craftsmen, builders, and end users all bring ideas to this project, making its impact more than the design and construction of the specific programs it houses.

A graduate of the Boston Architectural Center and the University of California, MARK S. GOLDMAN founded Onyx Construction / Design in Taos, New Mexico, in 1991, specializing in adobe construction and design.

The DreamTree Shelter in Taos, New Mexico, is first and foremost a place for homeless teenagers to be safe. It is also a place to embark on the journey toward a sustainable and dignified life. The three women who founded this nonprofit shelter, Joey Blue, Cami Hartman, and Kim Trieber, believe that the physical qualities of the shelter can be key elements in the healing of spirit, mind, and body. This priority of building a healthy community promotes the desire for sustainable architectural design, green materials, and construction practices wherever feasible. This essay analyzes both the good and the bad of the design and construction of the DreamTree facility, which, in addition to exploring and utilizing atypical methodologies, specifically stressed inclusion of local teenagers. My particular role in this project was as both architectural designer and construction supervisor.

The participation of unskilled young adults certainly did not diminish the roles of the architects, engineers, and construction professionals who also were key participants in the project. Rather, including teens in decision-making recognized that the building was going to be a home for teenagers. Regardless of their financial clout or how much time and complexity it would add to process, it was important to hear what teens had to say and to let them do what they could.

INITIAL STEPS

In 1998, New Mexico was the poorest state in the United States, with over one-quarter of its residents and over 40.5% of its children under the age of five living below the poverty level. In 1999, the U.S. Department of Housing and Urban Development (HUD) committed monies for the DreamTree Shelter based on a comprehensive proposal to provide an emergency shelter, transitional housing, and wilderness therapy program for youths. The HUD grant mandated an opening date within the year, yet provided funding for operations only, excluding using any funds for architectural design or construction. DreamTree partnered with the Rocky Mountain Youth Corps (RMYC), which maintains an AmeriCorps-financed construction crew for hire by nonprofits at reasonable rates. This partnership would provide training while also keeping the budget in check. A local philanthropist donated the land, with a 2,000-square-foot structure on it; he simply liked the idea that local teenagers would be building a facility for their peers.

I believe that Blue, Hartman, and Trieber trusted me with the responsibility to design and build the DreamTree Shelter in part because my family's background was similar to that of many of the kids who will use the project. As a teenager I could have personally benefited from a facility like the DreamTree Shelter. Also, I hold a New Mexico general contractor's license and have been a professional builder.

Before my work on the DreamTree Shelter I found it impossible to find meaningful projects in which to invest myself passionately. My experiences as a professional had led me to wonder if mainstream architecture in the United States was only for people from higher socioeconomic backgrounds than that from which I had come. I saw DreamTree as an opportunity to participate as architectural project manager in a grassroots community building, one that would allow rare procedural flexibility due to having neither the constraints of federal funding nor a university affiliation. My immediate goal was to create a functioning facility within the year, one with quality architecture, neither generically residential nor institutionally bland.

Northern New Mexico has a distinct regional architecture predating the United States by hundreds of years. The DreamTree steering committee desired a shelter that, while not rigidly historical, did initiate an aesthetic dialog with the older adobe buildings of Taos. Although it is sometimes surprising to visitors to New Mexico, adobe (unfired masonry) is still considered a premium construction material, with square foot costs often 20% above comparable stick-frame structures. Due to Taos's resort status, the cost of living there is the highest in the state, and it is common for native Taosenos to live in mobile homes, paying exorbitant heating bills while building luxury passive solar adobe vacation houses elsewhere in the state.

Contrary to many remote Western towns with eight thousand residents, Taos does have strict building codes and works hard to enforce them. In order to get DreamTree's hybrid building type approved and permitted, I took numerous trips down the Rio Grande Gorge to the state capital in Santa Fe to clarify issues with senior government building officials. We still had state building inspectors who were suspicious of our unusual project. Once we were completely shut down until yet another trip to Santa Fe produced stamped documentation stating that our original code analysis was correct.

We made a decision early on to seek design input from a wide variety of people, not just educated architects and engineers. Taos has a domestic violence shelter, and both their staff and clients were valuable for design input. Teens from Taos High School's teen issues class gave me further feedback while volunteering in the early stages of the project. Because we had no specific design prototypes to examine, we endeavored to be as inclusive as possible and try for the very best that we could do.

The initial architectural program for the DreamTree Project included spaces grouped into transitional and emergency shelter housing for sixteen teens, and office space. The New Mexico State Shelter Regulations prohibited housing independent living clients and emergency shelter clients within the same building, although they could be located on the same property. This bureaucratic mandate for separate structures actually worked well with the overall scale of the neighborhood. The design parti that Kim Trieber and I ultimately chose located the office functions in the west wing of the existing building, the emergency shelter in the east wing, and the transitional housing in the new structure to be located on the site. All three components would share use of a prominent circular space or "round room" addition. Here in the Southwest, round rooms are held to be sacred forms by the native Pueblo peoples. Our round room quickly became the image and guiding spirit of the design. At over twenty feet high it is visible from all angles. Exterior spaces for extensive organic gardens, a private outdoor porch, and courtyards were also part of the primary needs.

INTO CONSTRUCTION

On the day the property was transferred to the DreamTree Project, we held a ceremony on the site to celebrate the future community entity. Anglos, Latinos, Native Americans, and African Americans of a wide age span gathered around a small fire. A Native American ritual was performed there with reverence. Instead of responding to the spiritual nature of the ceremony, I was at that time feeling the immense pressure of many people's dreams resting on my shoulders. Later on, during the construction phase, I pinned up in the center of the building a quote from Christopher Alexander's *A Pattern Language*: "People cannot maintain their spiritual roots and their connection to the past if the physical world they live in does not also sustain these roots." I, along with all the worker-participants, would pass that message repeatedly during the day. I always felt energized when reading those words.

TOP: DreamTree provided an opportunity for homeless young adults to make design decisions and help build their new home. ABOVE: DreamTree shelter, south elevation.

TOP: The construction used traditional methods of the Taos area including adobe, canales, vigas, and latillas.
ABOVE: Entrance to the mud plaster "cubby" retreat cave.

The existing structure on the site—once housing the Northern New Mexico Midwifery Center, witness to over one thousand births—was gutted and its shell reused; however, the extensive programmatic needs of the shelter required more than triple that square footage. All the walls of the new construction are adobe, and in one of our seemingly endless series of cost-cutting measures, we built them using a state-of-the-art, mobile adobe pressing machine on loan from a local developer. This nearly $200,000 John Deere diesel-powered machine converted a sixty-ton pile of adobe dirt into precise ten-by-fourteen-by-four-inch bricks at a rate of nine each minute, costing only eighteen cents each compared to eighty-five cents to purchase the same size of sun-dried commercial ones. The cost to lay all 4,800 blocks would have been prohibitive without RMYC personnel, who did the major portion of the masonry along with volunteers from Taos High School's teen issues class, DreamTree staff, and even a local minister.

I once heard Scott Evans of RMYC say to his crew, "This project is not designed to be easy to build; don't get discouraged." The curved walls, rare ninety-degree angles, and twenty-four-foot-diameter round room would have been challenging for veteran "adoberos," let alone the teenagers, most of whom had never before held—let alone laid—an adobe brick. There were some problem areas that we had to tear down and rebuild, yet the walls went up, they are solid, and the unusual geometry routinely receives compliments. We created walls without cutting trees, walls that load the interior with sixty tons of valuable thermal mass. I believe the sense of accomplishment and empowerment that filled the builders of this stage were well worth any extra time that was required.

The interior design details of the shelter are visually rich yet were not expensive to build. When estimates for professional work came in too high, I trained the staff to do the soft, organic-feeling, three-coat plaster with deep bullnose details around interior windows. Vigas (peeled logs) for roof joists came from local forests, while other custom wood interior details were built on-site from material recycled from the Midwifery Center. We even created a "cubby," a little cavelike retreat off the living room, delicately finished by a local artisan with a local mud plaster containing large, reflective mica flakes. Paint schemes were, surprisingly, some of the most divisive decisions of the entire project. Some staff and teens liked what I thought were aggressive color treatments. I brought articles from professional journals discussing emotionally calming color combinations appropriate for group settings. The staff consulted their experts, the teenagers, and insisted on semitransparent, multilayered, strong colors with stenciled highlights. I have observed an interesting polarization of responses to the paint, with younger persons tending to be the enthusiastic constituency.

Some of what I consider the most vital design ideas were initiated by teens or workers, not the design professionals. The initial sketch idea for the cubby was brought in on notebook paper by Todd Thompson, a lead carpenter. Ben, a recent Taos High School graduate, drawknife-peeled some logs lying around the property and found them to be a beautiful local cedar, uniquely twisted. After a ride through the car wash in the bed of my truck, they are now featured in two prominent locations. James, a resident of the transitional housing program, expressed interest in making bookshelves for his bedroom. His simple, somewhat reserved freehand drawing gave me no indication of how passionately he would throw himself into the actual construction. At first I worked with James, showing him how to use the table saw and router. He proceeded to sand the recycled wood beautifully, becoming literally caked with sawdust, and he added some delicate decorative fins to the base.

I have been witness to many transformative events during the construction process. Willie, another transitional housing resident, assisted with the forming and pouring of the concrete bond beam on the round room. He took his job of reading the transit very seriously. By the end of a day of pouring concrete into the overhead forms, Willie's clothes, usually immaculate, were thoroughly splattered and soaked with concrete, yet he seemed to virtually glow with pride. Scott, the RMYC crew leader, has come back on his own time and volunteered skilled construction services. Juan, a RMYC crew member, confided to me about wanting to become a building contractor. Other teens on the RMYC work crews told me how exciting it was to learn the techniques to build a house of their own.

Whatever the response one has to the specific architectural character of the DreamTree shelter, I know it has become part of the community in a way that feels right. The job site is on a busy road; the evolution of its earthen forms are a changing public display. There was such interest in it that a well-attended mid-construction open house and fund-raiser allowed townspeople an opportunity to explore the job site accompanied by good food and live music. Creating this group residence has brought together wealthy real-estate developers (the donors of the project), homeless teens, high school students, social workers, Native American, Latino, and Anglo construction workers, architects, engineers, merchants, and countless others.

RECOGNIZING LESSONS

Was the project a success? In early 2001, the partially completed shelter went into operation, meeting the HUD deadline. To date, the construction costs have totaled sixty-eight dollars per square foot, which is significantly less than two-thirds of the market rate to build a comparable structure. The level of stress has continued to be high, however, mainly due to the constant fund-raising and searching for less expensive ways to get things built. I routinely change construction details, to the frustration of the workers, as alternate materials are donated or located at a discount. For example, the round room was first planned as straw-bale, then became an experimental sprayed cementitious material, then conventional sun-dried adobe, and eventually was built out of pressed adobe.

Expensive tools, including new laser surveying instruments, have been stolen from the job site even in daylight. Work has fallen behind schedule. Budgets frequently overrun expectations. Ironically, the most significant conflict did not involve any of the teenagers, but rather a mechanical contractor, who is threatening a lawsuit over a payment dispute.

The partnership between the DreamTree and the Rocky Mountain Youth Corps continues to grow stronger. Youths from the RMYC have ended up living in the transitional housing program. DreamTree also has some current staff who are RMYC-placed community service personnel. A mural in the office is currently being painted by an ex-RMYC worker, Laurel Bastian, who was first exposed to DreamTree by performing service work there.

Working on the DreamTree project in the paradigm of inclusiveness was, simply put, complicated and often frustrating. The positive results here seemed proportional to the effort put into the design and construction process. Including teenagers in this process has had many positive attributes, the major shortcoming being the extended time for the construction to take shape in comparison to having a professional crew. I am, however, not sure that it would have been significantly quicker had we assembled a group of inexperienced adults to build the DreamTree Shelter. There certainly would be little difference in the final product.

TOP: Ceiling of spruce logs in round room. ABOVE: Stucco exterior of round room nearing completion.

I often evaluated the DreamTree Shelter against a domestic violence shelter here in Taos that was built with a substantial HUD Community Development Block Grant. I was involved with the initial planning and ultimate construction of this shelter, and viewed DreamTree as a response to that experience. The domestic violence shelter was built at a much higher square-foot cost and utilized a metal frame structure with conventional interior finishes. The architect, general contractor, and major subcontractors were all from urban Albuquerque, and thus opportunities for local input were limited, and any opportunity for rural community building was clearly lost.

The design-build process—as used at the DreamTree Shelter, at least—was not intended to create future architects or builders; it was meant to forge community relationships. On the day that I assisted an elder from the Taos Pueblo, a sustainable community since ca. 1200 AD, in a ceremony blessing the DreamTree Shelter and its future residents, I reflected on the enthusiasm of the multicultural staff. Not only had we really created a place for homeless teenagers to be safe, but we had also built a home in which they could live with genuine pride.

MOBILE STUDIO
MARALEE GABLER

While over one hundred communities have the benefit of local architecture schools, and a few others have the benefit of Community Design Centers, most have neither and have little access to architectural or planning expertise. Despite its limits, the mobile studio can establish effective working relationships and make clear contributions to the underserved.

MARALEE GABLER acted as the Johnsonburg project manager at the Hamer Center for Community Design Assistance at The Pennsylvania State University.

The traditional fee structure of design services prohibits services to many, even among those who do have access to architectural expertise. One method of addressing these communities is described in this essay through the model of a mobile studio. While this model does not allow for a long-term relationship with a community (suggested by Rex Curry in his essay), it does provide a design process that includes the community and has better potential for understanding than the technical "expert" who travels in for a short time and then leaves. Despite its limits the mobile studio can establish effective working relationships and make clear contributions to the underserved.

I helped develop the Mobile Studio through the Hamer Center for Community Design Assistance, an outreach unit of the Pennsylvania State University.[1] The mission of the Hamer Center was developed under the direction of Michael Rios through a participatory process involving a nationwide survey of community design centers; a statewide survey of over 500 individuals, including members of county planning commissions, public agencies, nonprofit organizations, and citizen groups; and interviews with community representatives, faculty, and extension agents. From this process, we quickly realized that some community issues were going to be difficult to tackle in a studio setting over the course of a semester, let alone in-house at the Hamer Center. We thought that if there was a way to harness the knowledge, skills, and talents of a number of allied professionals and focus their collective energy for a period of time, we might begin to assist communities in prioritizing their design-related issues.

[1] The Hamer Center for Community Design Assistance would like to acknowledge and thank the Community Design Team of West Virginia University for sharing their experiences and materials during the creation of the Mobile Studio.

After surveying over forty-two university- and non-university-based centers and related programs, we found that many provide charettelike services to communities. Some focus on planning and providing socioeconomic recommendations, but few programs focus on these issues specifically as they relate to design. We saw an opportunity to bring design-related expertise to communities by coupling the strengths of our community design center and those of university faculty in related disciplines. We realized that many communities are inundated with master plans and are instead craving step-by-step attainable goals. One community we met requested that our team not provide yet another report that would just sit on a shelf and collect dust. We noted this request and began to ask ourselves how our team might be different.

PREPARING THE VISIT

We set out to create a way in which we could literally pick ourselves up and place ourselves *in* a community—living with people and working with them for a period of time. Make no mistake—the success of such a gesture would rely a great deal on the ability of our team to quickly absorb and assess all that we could, to provide meaningful and realistic recommendations. We knew that this would require an incredible amount of community organization ahead of time, so that each moment we would spend with the community would be meaningful. We asked ourselves, "What would I need to be able to show up somewhere I had never been, meet people I had never met, and provide them attainable, personal, and purposeful recommendations, within a day?" We made lists that included everything from places to sleep and food to eat to background materials and access to key buildings, sites, and people. We would need to coordinate these items, and many more, so that our team would be free to do their job.

We had to be sure that the community was ready for this type of service—their readiness would manifest in their ability to organize a host group to coordinate the visit itself. The host group would need to publicize the visit to the larger community, *before* the team arrived. Those active in community design know all too well that initiatives can fail without a broad base of support from the larger community. The host group needs to represent a diverse amount of interests in order to be able to initiate many of the recommendations, but they must also have the support of the larger community, including both decision makers and citizens, in order to complete the projects.

MEETING THE COMMUNITY

Our inaugural Mobile Studio was with the borough of Johnsonburg, Pennsylvania, a historic paper mill town of nearly 3,000 people. Johnsonburg is located in northwestern Pennsylvania, on a major transportation route between Canada and New York City, and is home to the Willamette Paper Mill. A new bypass was forcing the borough to make a series of tough design choices about its future.

The Johnsonburg Community Trust, a nonprofit community-based group, approached us for assistance in developing a streetscape plan for the downtown. The trust began a series of revitalization initiatives out of its concern for the new bypass, vacant downtown properties, and the migration of citizens to the surrounding suburbs. One of these initiatives was securing funds for streetscape improvements. We came to realize that Johnsonburg had a number of additional opportunities not only to improve its aesthetics, but also to better position itself economically and improve the quality of life of its residents. Resources such as the paper mill, the Clarion River, and Johnsonburg's location near a number of tourist destinations and natural resources provided a variety of environmental, recreational, employment, and housing opportunities. This made Johnsonburg an ideal candidate for a Mobile Studio visit.

We have worked with a number of talented, dedicated communities throughout the state of Pennsylvania, but the group that greeted us in Johnsonburg made a big impression on us. Representatives from a number of community, business, government and religious groups gathered to welcome us to the borough. Their enthusiasm and sincere desire and willingness to make their town a better place were something to behold. We knew this type of energy and commitment would be necessary for Johnsonburg to benefit from the ideas generated in a Mobile Studio visit.

APPLICATION PROCESS

Knowing that the vision we had for the Mobile Studio was to provide communities with short- and long-term design-related strategies, we designed the application process for the Mobile Studio to assist the community in organizing themselves for the visit and subsequent follow-through on the recommendations. The application asks the community to describe how they will organize and prepare for the team visit. The application requires a series of letters of support from different organizations, another step toward obtaining support from the larger community.

We have found that many communities are eager for assistance without realizing the level of time and commitment that change requires; therefore, we structured our application process to require a significant time commitment from the community. The application process and subsequent visit preparation can take up to nine months. This preparation includes forming a host committee; developing a publicity program to educate the larger

Team members work on concepts for the community greenway for Johnsonburg, Pennsylvania.

community about the visit; collecting background materials, base maps, and drawings; arranging interviews with community leaders and citizens; and other related activities.

We ask the host committee to arrange the food and lodging for the team. Citizens or local businesses often donate food, and local families, not hotels, must provide the lodging. Living with local families allows team members to truly be immersed in the community. As a team member, I have found that sharing this time with my host family taught me more about the community than I could have learned in months of study.

During the application process, we form a team with skills and knowledge specific to the community's needs by including faculty, extension agents, professionals, and graduate students in a variety of disciplines. We coordinate all aspects of the visit, making a less time-consuming commitment for the volunteers. After the visit, team members are given opportunities to provide feedback on the developing strategic projects report, but the primary donation of their time is the visit itself.

SETUP

Several details, such as supplies and technical support, must be carefully thought about and planned for, because there will not be time to figure these things out during the visit. As an inaugural Mobile Studio visit, there was a great deal of initial setup for Johnsonburg that has not been required in subsequent studios. We needed everything from drafting supplies and background materials to computer equipment. All the supplies for our Mobile Studio can be packed into the back of a fifteen-person van. First-year architecture students at Penn State designed a Mobile Studio cart to carry three wooden cabinets that hold all the drafting supplies. These cabinets form bases for three portable drafting tables also designed by the

Carts carry all of the Mobile Studio supplies and can be transported in a fifteen-person van.

students. These function well, but if we were to design them today we would not use the heavy one-half-inch plywood.

We accumulated several laptops, printers, scanners, and other equipment that allow the team to download images from digital cameras, access the Internet, or network information between groups. We found that while the virtual network is great in theory, unless there is technical support before, during, and after the visit, it is not worthwhile. Most often, team members use the computers for image manipulation and for PowerPoint presentations. We have also found that videotaping the entire visit, from initial interviews to the work sessions and final presentations, helps a great deal when assembling the final report.

THE VISIT

The visit itself usually lasts two to four days and is made up of a listening period and an intense working period. During the listening period, we introduce the team to the community through meetings with community leaders, a community tour, and discussions with local youth. During the working period the team develops a set of recommended strategies based on all the information gathered from the community.

The Johnsonburg Mobile Studio team arrived in Johnsonburg on a Thursday evening, and we met our respective host families. Friday morning we held back-to-back interviews with representatives of local governmental, environmental, educational, and citizen groups. In subsequent Mobile Studios, we have increased the time allotted for these interviews (we spent only fifteen minutes with each in Johnsonburg). We have also incorporated round-table discussions with more than one community member; this is an effective way for the team to hear many viewpoints, and it also begins the dialogue among community members that is such an important part of facilitating change. Following lunch, we took a guided tour of the community, followed by a work session at the local high school, where students presented their visions and assessment of the community through a photo essay they developed prior to the visit. In this way, we had an opportunity to understand the community from their perspective; the discussion ranged from social activities to crime to the future of Johnsonburg. In Johnsonburg, as well as other Mobile Studio visits, we are always amazed at the perception and honesty of the youth in regard to what is going on in their communities. After this meeting, we had a private dinner, followed by an evening work session to brainstorm the recommendations that we would develop Saturday.

Johnsonburg Mobile Studio team members discuss issues with Johnsonburg youth.

From eight A.M. to five P.M. Saturday, we worked in groups, each focusing on one of four main areas: entrances, downtown, a greenway along the Clarion River, and community building and networking. When we finished our work, we set up for a potluck dinner and town meeting. A group of high school students presented their thoughts to the community to kick off this meeting, which was attended by over one hundred citizens. Then team members summarized each group's recommendations. Finally, the meeting was opened up for questions and interaction between team members and community members. This allowed us to obtain feedback to be used in the final recommendations. Community members were given Post-it notes so they could attach comments directly on the drawings presented by the team.

In the months following the visit, the Hamer Center refined the team's recommendations into a report that detailed a list of ten to twenty strategic projects. Projects range from those that can be accomplished in a matter of days to those involving multiyear initiatives. A Mobile Studio visit, as we envisioned it, is not fully successful until a community begins to implement the recommendations. One way to ensure this is to follow up with communities after the team visit. In this way, a Mobile Studio visit can be the beginning of a longer-term relationship between a community and the design center. Projects that result from a Mobile Studio visit can become community-based design projects involving faculty, students, professionals, and center staff.

ESSENTIAL ELEMENTS

There are three key logistical elements without which the Mobile Studio could easily become the generator of just another "report."

PUBLICITY. Community support before, during, and after a visit is crucial to the success of the Mobile Studio. Publicity should include initial education on the purpose of the Mobile Studio; we often suggest that town meetings and community organizational meetings become starting places to begin this education process. Local newspapers, radio stations, organizational newsletters, merchants, and restaurants may be willing to post fliers or make announcements about the process. The public outreach component should include the purpose of the Mobile Studio, why the community wants a visit, examples of what the team might study during a visit, how the community interacts with the team, and why it is important to think about and plan for how the community will grow and change.

TIME. Working with the community to prepare for the visit and coordinating the team and the visit itself, as well as the final report and follow-up, require a considerable amount of staff time and resources. Similar programs in other parts of the country have dedicated one or more people full-time to these types of projects. For the Johnsonburg Mobile Studio, we had two staff members with other responsibilities split the tasks of organizing equipment and supplies, making logistical arrangements with the community, collecting background data, and compiling a final report.

FOLLOW-UP. Even communities such as Johnsonburg, which has a very active citizen's group, may have trouble getting started on the team's recommendation. The final report should not only present the rationale for the projects but also outline key resources, funding opportunities, tasks, and priorities. However, the report can only go so far. We found that designing our final reports much like a "how-to" booklet, as well as assisting the community in starting a project, can help them understand how to organize and tackle future projects. In Johnsonburg, Hamer Center staff helped the community to organize their first downtown tree planting. Over the course of six months, a staff member worked closely with community members to refine the streetscape plan developed by the team, secure materials and volunteers, publicize the tree-planting date, and conduct a series of workshops for the planting crew. Over twenty-five adults, youth, business owners, Penn State Extension agents, and Hamer Center staff worked a full day in April 2001 to plant trees along downtown Market Street. While the Johnsonburg visit itself and the following tree planting can be viewed as a success in terms of Johnsonburg's initial request, we have come to realize that the real power behind the Mobile Studio is in the continued work with a community after a visit toward accomplishing their greater goals. We need to form a longer-term relationship with communities in order to help them enact any long-term change. When a community is confident about our commitment to them, and they are equally committed to working with us, we can develop a relationship in which they become partner and collaborator, perhaps even designer.

EXPANDING THE ROLE
OF THE ARCHITECT
M. SCOTT BALL

According to a 1996 report by the Carnegie Foundation, 22% of students enrolled in architecture schools went into architecture to "help improve communities." Many of these graduates find they have to leave the traditional path of architecture to fulfill this goal.

M. SCOTT BALL is co-executive director of the Community Housing Resource Center, Inc. Before joining CHRC, he worked at Housing Operations and Management Enterprises (H.O.M.E.), Inc., in New Haven, Connecticut.

As progressively minded architects become involved in grassroots community-building efforts, we are likely to receive unanticipated invitations for our work, not all of which will require a drafting table. Invitations will be presented to us simply because the unique skills and knowledge base of our training are inherently valuable and relevant to all levels of society and all aspects of the built environment. Our ability to spot, solicit, and provoke such invitations will be critical to the process of negotiating a community-building role for our profession. In applying our skills to society's needs in new ways, we will reinvent architecture. It is my hope that in so doing architects will recognize why the well-being of all communities is inherently valuable to the health of our profession.

Communities solicit architects in two ways: specific requests are obvious, but unmet needs also ask to be addressed. The two forms of invitations act as catalysts for each other. Recognizing and addressing unmet needs can precipitate specific requests from a community, as its residents get to know us and understand the value of our skills. Proactive efforts at improving communities can thus seed the ground for professional expansion. As communities make specific requests, they can in turn lead us to a fuller understanding of our own capabilities and our own relevance in society. This entrepreneurial process then leads us to see other unmet needs and, hopefully, address them and thus provoke further invitations. Through this process we join with communities in learning that architecture is relevant.

Somehow our profession has not yet translated these opportunities into actions. Our tendency to huddle within safe institutional boundaries has interrupted the call and response between architects and communities and has created a removed and debased version of our profession. We have developed a stunting tendency to look to our fixed institutional shape first and then try to find needs to serve within that underdeveloped shape, rather than look to community needs and adjust our institutions to serve them. Our inwardly focused approach to our profession has fostered the illusion that architecture is something closed, finite, and predetermined. Architecture has become an idol that mesmerizes and immobilizes architects. We have forgotten that architecture is inseparable from culture and social structures, and we are in danger of bureaucratically cloistering ourselves into irrelevance.

Our profession can be brighter than that. Architecture is the sum total of what architects have done in the past and are doing in the present—and there is much that needs to be done. We focus on edifice, but architecture itself is whatever percolates out of our activity as trained architects. Invitations are everywhere for us to step back out into a broad section of society, if we would show a willingness to reinvent ourselves and allow the profession to percolate once again.

BEING USEFUL

In 1999, I received an invitation to work with the Community Housing Resource Center (CHRC), a community development corporation in Atlanta, Georgia. CHRC manages a housing hotline, operates a centralized intake system for Atlanta's home repair and rehab programs, and keeps track of a large network of affordable housing providers and neighborhood-based organizations. This job has allowed me to focus on the basic human need for shelter and has provided a starting point to create a community-based practice. CHRC is located on the south side of the city, and I am of a profession, a race, and an economic class that rarely stray from the north side. I hope that elaborating on my own

Political advocacy, such as fighting predatory lending, is one role of architects.

experience may be of use to others in spotting invitations and openings for architects where they can already be found, and in provoking specific invitations in places where we perceive a need.

Being useful, in whatever form that takes, has been a great way for me to get involved with communities as a young architect. Directly out of architecture school, I interned in a mid-sized firm and volunteered at CHRC at night and on weekends. This volunteer work was easy to get because the need was there and because most community meetings take place after regular business hours, making them easy to accommodate into a work schedule. Spending time in the office and participating in meetings provided a great vantage point for surveying the community and for locating opportunities to interact with it.

FINDING A ROLE IN THE COMMUNITY

I was hired at CHRC to create and direct an Emergency Repair Program because the staff felt that I was qualified to fix houses. While recognizing that this was not a commission on par with designing a new art museum, it was a specific request for my skills, and the utter usefulness of the job appealed to me. I was willing to let go of some of my preconceptions about what I should be doing with my Yale architecture degree (museums, monuments, and the like) and simply take suggestions from others as to where I might be useful. My willingness to lend a hand where asked gave the communities I work with a chance to assess my skills and abilities. If I had been too insistent about what I would and

An existing circuit breaker becomes a design element in an interior.

would not do, I do not think it would have been possible to develop the current role I have with the community.

I quickly came to realize that I was, in fact, uniquely qualified for the work I was asked to do and, what is more, that I was not overqualified. Many of the homes CHRC was to serve had serious, long-term deterioration problems. Dealing with these problems would require an understanding of the interrelation of many systems and judgments about where to start and stop the work so that the most benefit could be derived from extremely limited budgets. The staff members who interviewed me for the job were concerned that the trade-based construction backgrounds of most candidates were ill suited for the work. I was the only architect to apply for the position, and the people at CHRC judged that an architect's knowledge base, being more general and holistic, would be more useful to them than the specific and compartmentalized skill sets of people who had experience only with trade work.

As director of emergency repair for two and a half years, I inspected approximately 1,600 low-income homes, many of which had life-threatening conditions. I oversaw the repair and rehabilitation of about half of these houses, averaging about $4,000 per home, and I learned a great deal about architecture in the process. This rehab work was a lot like studio design work: a process of nudging and tweaking projects in the right direction. I learned how to consider the needs of the clients, the limits of the budget, and the state of the house, and then in "ishes" (that is, get it sturdyish here, flatish there, straightish over here) to nudge the house back into a stable and functional state. There is no better training for this work than the give-and-take process of studio design work.

TOP: Side view of the design-build house. ABOVE: Will Danielson in loft of design-build house during construction.

I like architecture magazines—the glossy kind. I am a sucker for the shiny and bendy. My work in South Atlanta has not diminished my attraction to cutting-edge design, even of the most abject, superficial, aesthetic variety. I love it.

But many of my neighbors are put off by innovative residential design. It is not a dislike for design in itself—car modifications in my neighborhood are often thoughtful and many times outrageous—but when it comes to homes, people are much more conservative about appearance. Architects may be responsible for some of this. It does not help that most of my nonprofit housing colleagues have worked on long-anticipated, community-initiated projects in which the architect drove the design in a direction they did not like. Lacking the budget to start over with a more responsive architect, communities generally have had to settle for what they are given in these situations. In many communities, this has been their only experience with the architectural profession, and this, of course, creates resentment and distrust. But architects are not solely responsible for the conservativeness of the housing market. Architects are simply not around enough to warrant the level of distrust they often confront in the field of community development.

My willingness to lend a hand where asked did develop trust with the community and a bit more license to push design than an "outside" firm would have. I did not simply prefer better design from an aesthetic viewpoint, but understood the practical benefit of bringing innovative design to community service. Cutting-edge design is very valuable to affordable-housing efforts because it allows the architect to set aside preconceptions and approach problems with fresh eyes. Given the rate at which building materials and construction processes are evolving, and the rate that use patterns of homes are changing, it is necessary to reevaluate expectations on a regular basis. Innovative design has this eminently practical dimension. Plus, it looks good.

I am now co-executive director of CHRC. I have delegated emergency repair to others, and am focusing on policy issues and starting a series of new construction, demonstration homes. I am finding that many manufacturers of building products are eager to get homes built that demonstrate the virtues of their new product lines. There seems to be a niche for our organization to do these showcase projects in a thoughtful and publicity-generating manner. I am able to do these homes with the support of my board and the broader community because I have spent time in the trenches of emergency repair. Through this time, I have built trust and negotiated allowances to pursue things that are out of the ordinary. The "do-gooder" reputation the organization has developed through its repair work is also attractive to building product manufacturers interested in developing new markets.

But perhaps most importantly, time in the trenches has enabled me to spot openings for design progress. Through the Emergency Repair Program, CHRC has accumulated volumes of photographic documentation showing that Levittown-style tract housing does not fare well over time in the South. In the nearly subtropic climate of Atlanta, there are many environmental forces hostile to the stick-built, sheetrocked, carpeted boxes in which we have grown accustomed to dwell. While many of my colleagues may be initially uncomfortable with the thought of innovative residential design, it usually only takes a few moments of flipping through the photo documentation in the emergency repair files to overcome their apprehensions. I have found that there is a greater willingness to consider the new when it is put into the perspective of what is not working in the old. The documentation of building failures helps to convince folks of the utter usefulness and practicality of new design

CHRC creates an affordable home-ownership opportunity through a design-build house.

approaches. And, of course, it has not hurt me one bit as a designer to have seen and dealt with these problems firsthand.

THE EXPANDED ROLE

Through my work with CHRC, I have been able to develop an architectural practice as an integral member of a community by being open to nonestablished roles and advocating as an insider for the more established ones. The primary catalyst for my practice has been my willingness to be useful first, and then figure out how my usefulness is architectural. I rely heavily on invitations and value the possibilities that they reveal for architecture to find relevant expression.

I have yet to chase an unexpected thread that did not in some way bring me back to architecture with a newfound appreciation for the skills and insights provided by my professional training. This is not missionary work—I am getting a lot out of it. The language of architecture lives and breathes today solely because it is inherently intriguing and relevant. Opportunities to apply and develop our skills are everywhere around us. With this abundance of invitations, we are not dependent on the latest iteration of the institutional vessel to parsimoniously ladle a moribund version of tradition to future projects. We can simply use the rule of thumb that if it looks like it could use the help of an architect, it probably is architecture.

It would behoove us to discover how these invitations reveal our professional role—both to ourselves and to the general public. The tradition of architecture is rich and does not bind us to a set of safe, defensible, standardized, bureaucratic contracts and procedures. Instead, we are licensed to designate as architecture all activity that lends expression to our unique set of skills. Tradition encourages us to pursue unanticipated invitations, to be included in the work of community building, and to structure our profession only as required to make sense out of our engaged involvement. There is no shortage of demand for our skills—we lack only the confidence to allow these demands to structure and include us.

COMMUNICATION
ANDREA DIETZ

The hopes and dreams of many communities are dependent on the visioning skills of design and the practical skill of construction budgeting. Architects are trained to provide both services, and thus can play an important role in community projects.

TUCCA
Community Center

ANDREA DIETZ was project designer of the TUCCA community center. She has a Bachelor of Science in Architecture (2000) from the University of Virginia and was an AmeriCorps VISTA member with Design Corps in 2000–2001.

As banks, foundations, and government sources need to know what they are funding, design proposals and construction budgets for community projects are almost always required before any funds can be accessed. Architects can play the critical role of giving these projects life and a realistic path for success by helping at this early stage of planning.

MY INTRODUCTION TO TUCCA

My architecture diploma in hand, I stepped off the traditional preprofessional degree path and onto one of service as a VISTA volunteer through Design Corps. I hoped to carry the benefits of architecture and design to those who needed it the most—low-income and less-privileged people—to my first assignment with The United Christian Community Association (TUCCA). Taylor, Alabama, is an isolated community, miles from the nearest town, consisting of random houses sporadically placed in a landscape of rolling red-earth flatlands, catfish ponds, pothole-pocked roads, and evergreens. It is a fractured community, led by conflicting church congregations, with the added barriers of segregation, poverty, dwindling population, and economic depression. But amid the discouragement is hope in TUCCA's extraordinary assembly of African-American churches, a group with a vision to tear down the walls of division and build walls of communion instead.

We build a simple roadside community information board to physically mark our project and to facilitate communication.

TUCCA began as an effort to empower and organize the community, and their commitment led them to purchase forty-five acres of raw land where they could realize their physical dreams. With a great deal of hope but little technical knowledge, TUCCA engaged Design Corps to help them transform the land into their vision. This occurred over a series of projects that helped build a working relationship with Design Corps as well as faith that change could indeed occur.

I was first introduced to TUCCA on paper—to the people of Taylor through demographic and statistic studies, to my project through the master plan created before I began my VISTA term. I understood that the task before me was a challenge, a balancing act between despair and potential. But I did not grasp the magnitude of my charge until I actually met the situation at a high school homecoming football game in Taylor, where there was only silence after a big touchdown—no cheering, no clapping. My primary community contact, Andrew Williams, explained that this was because no pride existed in the community, even in their homecoming court. It was a culture shock and a warning of the great differences that existed between me and the group I hoped to serve.

The next morning arrived in striking contrast, filled with hope. I attended, for the first time, TUCCA's monthly meeting and was encouraged by their ambitious optimism: "We must tear down the walls that divide and build anew walls to unite." These simple words from a sermon had inspired a handful of people to pool their resources, buy land, and independently prepare it for construction—clear trees, lay roads, carve out a lake, and plan for commerce, education, recreation, and residence in the form of a community center, barbecue pavilion, softball field, nature trail, housing development, and basic utilities such as sewage and water systems. Their lofty goal was to rebuild their community, literally and figuratively, into a happier, stronger place. It was in this world of opposite extremes, hopelessness versus ambition, that I assumed the struggle to make a difference.

Design Corps' first step was to help organize the site into a community plan of twenty-two houses, which were arranged around the perimeter of the land, allowing for a common green space in the middle. Design Corps then helped gain the necessary approvals to create a dam and lake in the center of the common space.

With these planning preliminaries accomplished and the lake beginning to fill, the first actual building took place. A team of seven from Design Corps visited Taylor to construct a community information board along the highway in front of the TUCCA property. My design of this simple structure allowed TUCCA members to communicate about progress and meetings, and invited the greater community to post "lost pet" and "for sale" fliers. It also encouraged travelers to slow and observe the changes taking place down the hill.

The second building project was a barbecue pavilion to house the annual TUCCA picnic. Barbecue has developed into quite an art form and source of pride in the region, and Lesli Stinger, the Design Corps designer of the pavilion, spent a lot of time studying the social aspects of and local precedents for cooking structures. Her design combined the pavilion with a "social path" connecting the cooking pit, serving area, and seating areas. Stinger was challenged to communicate building instructions to the community volunteers who would be building most of the structure. As she knew her curving structure would appear complex to community members, she used some larger-scale models to show that the actual construction was simple. This proved effective, certainly more effective than traditional construction documents, which communicate between architects and builders in a very technical way. With the growth of Habitat for Humanity and other programs where laypeople are involved in construction, a need is growing for this type of alternative construction instructions as well.

To build the pavilion, the seven Design Corps visitors worked with a rotating community team that gradually gained enthusiasm as well as construction knowledge. At the end of a week, two bays were completed, and the posts for the remainder were set. It was gratifying to us that the community itself completed the rest of the structure within six weeks and that they overcame the challenges of a unique structure.

THE TUCCA COMMUNITY CENTER

The final building that Design Corps addressed was a highly ambitious community center, which I designed. The building included nonprofit activities such as computer training, a library, and a daycare center; business activities such as a barbershop and a restaurant; and recreation areas such as a basketball court and swimming pool. I did not want to discourage TUCCA's dream, but I knew this wish list required much more than designing a building to house these activities. Prioritizing and planning for staged construction that held some financial reality became a huge challenge for me. But learning to communicate with non-architects turned out to be my biggest challenge. Fresh out of school, armed with my studio vocabulary and jury presentation skills, I charged forward—and tripped. I realized neither the breadth nor the hindering power of the gap in communication between the architect's academic world and the "outside" everyday world until I was forced to span it myself.

At my first TUCCA meeting, I could not prioritize the elements in the community center program and discuss their proximities without using terms that I had learned in school but that the community members did not understand. In my attempt to avoid these terms my sentences became overly complex; instead of saying "the building program" I said "the different rooms inside a building," instead of "proximity" I used "the rooms you want next to

TOP: Model of the barbeque pavilion, showing how socializing is expressed as a path. ABOVE: After we completed these two bays with local volunteers, the community completed the rest in six weeks.

each other versus the rooms you want far away from each other," and so on. My mouth was a jumble of archi-speak; I had to repeat everything. By the time I was ready to present the three potential schemes I had prepared, my audience was either too exhausted or too doubtful to offer a response.

I approached my second meeting with a metaphor connecting the walls of TUCCA's motivational sermon to the foundation walls of their new community center. I suggested that the physical walls could bring people together as they supported a unifying overhead tent, or giant roof structure, that would house the rooms of their community center. The audience applauded the poetry. Encouraged, I moved on to the concept of three phases of construction: first, creating the space with the walls and the tent; second, filling in the space with the most important rooms; and third, finishing with the "luxury" items. Everyone in the room nodded in agreement. But when it came to discussing logistics, I lost them again: "You have a fairly steep site here, a thirty-six-foot drop in elevation from the front to the back. So, these walls will act as the retaining walls that prepare the site for construction. And, to minimize expense, I've located them to follow the lines of the natural topography." Silence. "You mean, we need walls to hold back the earth? We're going to make the walls work with our hill?" I attempted to clarify my thoughts with drawings and models, but my abstract creations were just as useless as my specialized words.

By the third meeting, I was desperate for participation and input, longing even for the once-dreaded desk critique, aching to design something more than a guess at my client's ideals. Before congregating, I mailed TUCCA members a hands-on model consisting of a felt base representing the site and cubes (attached with Velcro) representing the rooms: classrooms, commercial units, gymnasium, locker rooms, library/computer lab, office, meeting room, recreation rooms, restrooms, swimming pool. I sent the model in a suggested arrangement but asked the TUCCA members to play with and rearrange the components to their liking. I arrived at the meeting to find the model untouched. I told them that I needed their criticism to get ideas, to make this community center theirs. They responded that they trusted me, but that did not convince me that they understood the building design that was taking shape.

My next effort for input was a four-question, anonymous survey asking TUCCA members what they liked about the community center design, what they did not like, what they would change, and what they thought best represented their community. Feedback started to come in, but still reflected some confusion. When I asked how they liked the model, one answer commented on the model material itself rather than the design it represented. Other comments did start to express approval. One, for example, said that they would not change anything (except the addition of a snack bar at the pool).

CONCLUDING MY PROJECT

For the conclusion of my VISTA year, I built on this beginning to learn how I could gain TUCCA's input. As I crafted the plans, sections, elevations, perspectives, and models of TUCCA's community center, I devoted myself to capturing artistically the spirit of an inspiring people.

One of the problems in developing communication had been that I made my presentations during meetings with many other agenda items. The short time slot I was given did not encourage extensive two-way communication, but rather just a presentation. Realizing this, I requested a specific meeting to discuss the community center. I arranged to test my final concepts on Andrew Williams, one of the TUCCA leaders, before tackling the entire group. In so doing, I made the biggest leap in participatory design of my entire Design Corps career.

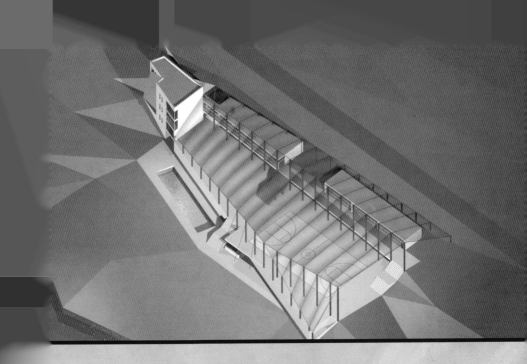

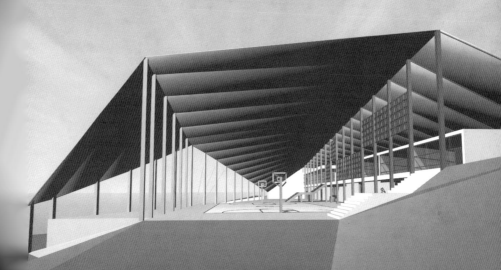

TOP: Axonometric view of TUCCA Community Center showing the concept of rebuilt walls and the inclusive tent. ABOVE: The tent provides inexpensive recreation space simply by shielding the harsh sunlight while allowing breezes to pass through.

This run-through allowed me to make improvements before the group presentation. For, as I failed miserably in communicating my ideas to Williams and succeeded only in overwhelming him with material, I learned from our meeting how to talk, what to edit, and what to show the members of TUCCA. Plus, through Williams I gained a community voice, someone familiar enough with my objective that he could translate any remaining archi-speak to the others.

The next day, ironically and finally, I communicated. I walked slowly through four points, drawing each on the board as I progressed, stopping between each until I got a reaction and waiting for Williams to interpret. I realized sometimes we have to shut up. At the very end of the meeting, as an aside, I revealed the full scope of my "actual work." In this way I established a basic understanding with and gained the undivided attention of the members of TUCCA. I learned that while they viewed my scheme as beautiful and incredible, they were not convinced that it was entirely realistic, even though it was the form of the dreams they had shared with me. Together we paced out my plans on their site and I left them to weigh their ambitious plans and maybe to readapt them if their dreams were too great.

Members of TUCCA, with Andrew Williams and Andrea Dietz at center, pace out the community center on their site.

The story of the TUCCA community center is not a fairy tale; it is not even a story of success. But it is, perhaps, a story of progress. TUCCA is one step closer to the realization of their community center. Through the visuals I left with them, they have a tool with which to seek grant funding, should they decide to pursue the next step. Ideally, they even have a little something about which to dream.

As for me, I have learned a valuable lesson: If architecture truly is to be a social art, then the architect must truly be for the people—speaking for the people, crafting for the people, designing for the people, communicating, connecting, including. Maybe that knowledge is what will make all the difference.

4 / RELATING SOCIAL NEEDS TO DESIGN

THE ROLE OF THE CITIZEN ARCHITECT
SAMUEL MOCKBEE

Much contemporary architecture is undemocratic and exclusive. Samuel Mockbee explains how Auburn University's Rural Studio aspires to the role of the citizen architect to make architecture more creditable and socially relevant.

SAMUEL MOCKBEE founded Auburn University's Rural Studio with D. K. Ruth in 1993 and headed it until his death in 2001. This text is transcribed from remarks he made at the first Structures for Inclusion Conference, held at Princeton University on October 7, 2000.

Walt Whitman said the most obscene word in the English language was "exclusion," such as exclusion from a country club or a gated community, or from the democratic process. The main purpose of the Auburn Rural Studio is how architectural practice might be challenged with a deeper democratic purpose of inclusion. Our focus is on the role an architect should or would play in providing quality of life to all citizens, both underserved and overprivileged. This role should be given a purpose where architects stand for solutions that service a community's physical and social needs, and not just the complacent status quo. So the Rural Studio has turned to the study of what could make architecture more creditable through the role of the citizen architect.

The American economy is increasingly dependent upon advances in science and technology. Scientific research and knowledge has now become a power. Acknowledging this current popular notion, however, does not diminish the importance of the arts. Unlike science, the making and appreciation of art is integral to the fundamental values of the democratic principles. The role of the arts is similar to that of new ideas in science. The arts create and sustain new ways of discovering truth, beauty, and the moral sense in a culture. The study of science should be informed by arts and vice versa. The arts should hold the same prestige and influence as the sciences. In other words, it is equally important that the arts and sciences have access to the same democratic values, such as the freedom of expression and a moral sense, in order to reach the highest achievements.

There is a difference in how the two fields proceed in transforming the status quo of the actual world. Unlike science, art often begins anew by reinventing itself, by building upon a past principle and ethical relationship. These reoccurring relationships should approximately address the needs of each new generation's social, physical, political, aesthetic, and environmental issues of the day. It is this ability to reinvent itself that has inspired the Rural Studio to perform an educational role that is rooted in an organic relationship still found in the rural Black Belt of west Alabama. It is these reoccurring themes based on tradition, politics, manners, rituals, politics, courtships, friendships, status quo, and the values of the rural community that have inspired the work of the Rural Studio. And while the Rural Studio is purposefully located in the relative obscurity of rural Alabama, it is precisely the situation of people and place that stimulates and challenges an education that is real in itself, an ultimate comparison between the noble aspirations of American science and art.

Now I am the first to admit that architecture cannot alleviate all the social and physical woes of rural Alabama communities. But what is necessary is a willingness to seek solutions to the community in its own context and not from the outside. What is required is the perfect placement of abstract notions with the knowledge based on real human contact and personal realization applied to a people and place.

In creating architecture, and ultimately community, it should make no difference which economic or social type is served, as long as the status quo of the actual world is transformed by an imagination that creates a proper harmony for both the affluent and the disadvantaged. It seems to me that the most important consideration of architects is not the matter of a client's economic status, but the appropriateness of their exploration. Also, the most valuable thing I have learned in working with these extremes, both the very rich and very poor, is that what appears to be a disparity disappears into an honesty of spirit. It is their honest lifestyle that raises their status above the ordinary. Therefore, it is important that we give our attention to what are some basic issues regardless of time or place—not just questions of judgment, but questions of values and principles. All architects expect and hope that their

FACING PAGE FROM TOP: Lucy's House built by the Auburn University Outreach Studio in Mason's Bend, Alabama. The house is located near the first two houses built by the Rural Studio for the children's grandparents, in Mason's Bend. The new wall system is built on a slab and capped with wooden box beams. THIS PAGE FROM TOP: The Harris family in their living room. The main building material is remnant carpet samples layered and post-stressed onto threaded rods.

work will serve humanity and make a better world. That is the service that we should always be making. What the Rural Studio is interested in is the architect's place in society and the impact our profession has on public policy issues of education, transportation, law enforcement, health care, employment, and the environment—in other words, the role that architecture can play in improving the life in a rural community.

I do not believe that courage has left our profession. On the contrary, at the beginning of the twenty-first century, our profession is on the very verge of reinventing itself through technology and science. But we still tend to be narrow in the scope of our thinking and devoid of our moral responsibilities to warn and inform. In other words, we still have the duty to participate in the social, political, and environmental realities our communities are facing, and this requires architects to look beyond architecture toward an enhanced understanding of the whole to which it belongs. It takes a peering out at the contemporary landscape before commitments to nudge and cajole and inspire can be started, worked on, and accomplished.

Architecture more than any other art form is a social art, and for those of us who design and build, we must do so with an awareness of a more socially and physically responsive architecture. The practice of architecture not only requires the active individual participation in the profession, but it also requires active civic engagement. The architect's primary emotional connection should always be with place, and not just the superficial qualities of place, but the ethical responsibility of shaping the environment, of breaking up social complacency and energizing one's community. It is not prudent for the architect to sit back and rely on the corporate world, science, and technology experts to decide what problems to address. It is in our own self-interest to assert our ethical values and our talents as citizen architects.

I believe most of us would agree that American architecture today exists primarily within a thin band of elite social and economic conditions. So to me the question is really a matter of understanding appropriateness. I have worked with both the upper 1% and the lower 1%. And in working with these two most extreme poles, it seems to me there is much in common. For each, the challenge is the responsible distribution of appropriate resources for the individual, and for society as well. This is not the redistribution of resources, but the responsible and appropriate use of society's resources as a whole.

It has become extremely clear to me that if architectural education is going to play any role in improving the quality of life in a community, or to challenge the status quo and to make responsible environmental, social, and structural changes, I would have to work with that segment of the profession that would one day be in a position to redefine and reinvent our communities: students.

What we explore at the Rural Studio is how to place architecture into real human service. We are interested in what might prompt and make possible a process of entering a taboo landscape, in our case the economic poverty of the Deep South, and also develop a discourse beyond merely looking at the effects of poverty to how architects can step over the threshold of misunderstood values and discover the real needs of a neglected American family.

Hale County is the landscape that the students and myself find ourselves working in. It is a beautiful landscape, and it has a rich cultural history. If you look at Walker Evans's slides of Hale County from 1936 compared to today, you will see that not a goddamn thing has changed for some families. W. E. B. DuBois said at the end of the last century that the great challenge for the twentieth century would be to bring those up who had been left behind. Those who have been left behind are the invisible members of our family. Here we are in the twenty-first century, and we still have people living in these conditions.

Our primary mission is an academic program to get these architecture students out to deal with social and physical issues of a community. That is the mission. The fact that we end up building houses and community projects, that is the homework. Primarily what we do is build community projects. The sophomores build the houses. Then they can come back in their fifth year and do a thesis project.

These projects try to give us an American architecture without pretense. They remind us that we can be awed by the simple as equally as the complex. And if we pay attention, they will offer us a glimpse into what is essential to the future of American architecture: its inclusion of democratic principles.

SUSTAINABLE COMMUNITY PLANNING: PROTOTYPE FOR THE MOHAWKS OF KAHNAWAKE, QUEBEC

JULIA BOURKE

Recent small-scale efforts by Canadian First Nations communities, and both private and public sector professionals, have redefined the native housing crisis as a matter of process over product. This has resulted in new inclusionary models of community development, which are placing the First Nations at the forefront of Canadian housing innovation.

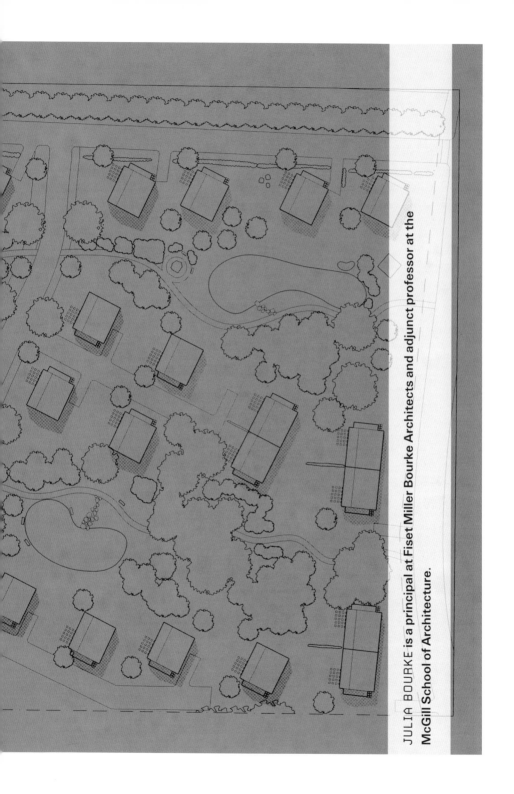

JULIA BOURKE is a principal at Fiset Miller Bourke Architects and adjunct professor at the McGill School of Architecture.

The housing crisis in Canadian First Nations communities is a problem of national proportion, regularly discussed but little understood. The subject of extensive political negotiations and regular media coverage, it is commonly identified as a matter of financing and measured in numbers of units built. Fifteen to forty minimum-cost bungalow-style tract houses are in fact constructed each year with government funding in each of hundreds of aboriginal communities nationwide. Most such territories are remote, recently established settlements with very limited access to materials and services, harsh weather conditions, and pressing social problems. In some cases, entire new towns are built from scratch in new locations, for "a fresh start." The construction budgets for the houses are minimal, and the planning, financing, and building processes are conventional.

The results, which do solve the short-term problems of overcrowding and lack of basic shelter, nevertheless fail to address more subtle and insidious issues of psychological and cultural dislocation, and long-term problems of housing dilapidation and community disintegration. The impact of these deceptively banal housing and planning strategies are tragically exaggerated in these fragile communities traditionally defined by intimate ties to extended families and the natural environment. Yet the alienation, social unrest, and significant health problems that are well documented here are firmly rooted in a general failure in housing construction across the North American continent. The impersonal neighborhood layouts, unhealthy building materials, poor water quality, inefficient energy sources, and substantial alteration of the landscape typical of these remote communities are in fact familiar qualities endemic to the North American suburban landscape.

A HOUSE IN KAHNAWAKE

One recent project in the Mohawk settlement of Kahnawake provides an alternative case study: while originated by a handful of individuals, it now counts among a growing number of initiatives encouraged by funding and technical support from researchers at the Canadian Mortgage and Housing Corporation (CMHC) and the Department of Northern and Indian Affairs.

Kahnawake, a territory of twelve thousand acres bordering the Saint Lawrence River and sandwiched among the suburbs of Montreal, Quebec, is in the unusual position of being located adjacent a major "southern" city. This proximity has allowed it to benefit from greater access to resources—professional, academic, and industrial—than other native communities. At the same time the territory has been dramatically scarred by large-scale infrastructure interventions generated by Montreal's adjacency—train and power lines, a major highway, and a shipping seaway that has largely cut the community off from the water. Kahnawake's population of over five thousand inhabitants is primarily housed in minimum-cost suburban tract housing fanning out from a small waterfront village in irregular clusters interspersed with forest and abandoned farmland. Approximately twenty-five new bungalows are built each year, in quarter-acre subdivisions of existing pockets of remaining "common land" remote from the village center. Qualifying homeowners (Mohawks without private land) are picked from a waiting list and allocated a $50,000 construction loan with which to construct a two- or three-bedroom house ($60,000 if they have $5,000 cash to contribute).

Kahnawake is one of a handful of independent Mohawk settlements dispersed in southern Quebec and Ontario as well as New York State. It is run by a locally elected Band Council with annual federal funding allocations, a structure typical of First Nations settlements. As I understand it, while Kahnawake's council has achieved a greater degree of political independence than many, its legitimacy continues to be a source of internal debate: it is without taxation power and officially disconnected from the traditional clan structure as represented by the longhouses.

Aerial view of Kahnawake Territory, Quebec.

KANATA 2000

The Kahnawake project, dubbed "Kanata 2000," began in 1998 when two Mohawk women, as coordinators of the Kahnawake housing and environment offices, obtained a federal "innovative housing" construction grant of Can$70,000, an amount that slightly exceeds the standard budget of $50–65,000 allocated to each household within the community. These two women, Eva Johnson and Iris Jacobs, pooled their knowledge of environmental health problems, their traditionalist values, and the activities of the housing department to identify a new healthy house prototype relevant to the community. Although their grant did not include funding for the design process, they managed to assemble a core team including local engineer Robert Deom, recent environmental science graduate Lynn Jacobs, outside environmental consultant Peter Kettenbeill, and my own firm, Fiset Miller Bourke architects, which specializes in affordable, ecological architecture and community planning.

The Kanata 2000 team proceeded with periodic participation by elected Band Council members, as well as the input of Cultural Center Director Kahnatakta Beauvais. CMHC provided funding as well as encouragement and technical support. From the beginning, instead of adopting the traditional consultant-client relationship, the respective team members established a collaborative approach in identifying and approaching potential funding sources as well as accomplishing the work. This was triggered in part by the clients' lack of financial resources, but was also fueled by their exclusive expertise in community matters coupled with their strong will to achieve autonomy from outside consultants. Although this participatory process sometimes tended to devalue the professionals' contributions, it was ultimately very fruitful on many levels.

A SUSTAINABLE CASE STUDY

Johnson and Jacobs saw the housing innovation grant as an opportunity to build an ecological house, an objective that resonated with traditional Mohawk values of the interdependence of man and nature and the necessity to act with the long term in view. The team's official mandate was to "to empower the community with the tools and models to choose a sustainable shelter and lifestyle." My own conviction that a sustainable house could not be designed in isolation led us to shift our work from the scale of an individual home to that of a sustainable neighborhood, and from technical and material design constraints to sociocultural, political, and economic issues. With the Band Council's promise of a ten-acre site, we proceeded with extensive predesign research.

The first research step was a report, produced by the Mohawk team members with limited technical input from the consultants. It gives a historical, cultural, and social overview of the community and broadly describes housing-related financial issues as well as the community's physical characteristics. It identifies and rates ecological systems and materials and also documents a community "focus group" on ecological housing: though poorly attended and very technical in focus, this meeting did serve to publicize the project and identify a handful of people potentially interested in housing alternatives. Additional public-ity was undertaken with radio spots, articles in the local press, coverage on the council web site, and an information booth at the local community center and festivals.

The report provided a stepping stone for further research. The value of sweat equity, or owner-built housing, briefly mentioned in the initial study as a common occurrence tradition-ally undertaken by extended families, led to a separate study concluding with guidelines for regulatory change and a sweat-equity component to the demonstration project. Kahnawake is in fact a community of builders: internationally recognized for their expertise in high-rise steel construction, community members also produce the local wood-frame housing, with skills in all trades with the exception of foundation work. A few informal telephone inter-views with self-builders led to home tours by the proud owners, and the collection of critical knowledge regarding homeowner preferences and the obstacles and pitfalls of sweat equity.

My own part-time role as adjunct professor at the McGill School of Architecture allowed me to enlist the assistance of graduate students from the Minimum Cost Housing Program to amplify the research. A user assessment conducted by students from a joint social sciences/housing initiative was more successful than the first report's focus group in identify-ing community needs. The students, whose own ethnic backgrounds (Palestinian, Lebanese, and Israeli) earned them easy acceptance by the Mohawk partners, were also well received in the community and conducted ten interviews with subjects varying in age, marital status, and gender. The study identified a general desire for privacy, space, flexibility, and limited maintenance costs. One interviewee highlighted the traditional importance of solar orientation in the daily rituals of living: greeting the morning sun from an eastern bed-room window, and gracing the evening meal with the presence of the setting sun. In the absence of a specific homeowner for the demonstration project, these issues became valu-able design criteria. Additional student work allowed us to more specifically identify physical characteristics of particular relevance to the design process. They undertook detailed map-pings of transportation, land use, topography, soil and vegetation, and population density as well as sketch and photo documentation of existing house types, renovation patterns, and streetscape characteristics.

THE MASTER PLAN

The master plan for the neighborhood consists of thirty-five single-family units on a flat ten-acre site flanking Kahnawake's main road and clustered around a central meeting house/day-care/community pool area. The land use strategies are designed to permit the preservation of family groupings, the nurturing of a community spirit, and the preservation of a link to nature. The housing is planned to facilitate home busi-nesses including retail, which, though common in the commu-nity, are not easily accommodated by the traditional bungalow.

Kanata 2000 master plan.

The layout promises both short- and long-term economies, and a significant increase in environmental quality on four basic levels. First, increased density and smaller roads create economy and intimacy. Second, houses are sited strategically to increase privacy and per-mit additions to individual homes as well as a future second home for extended families.

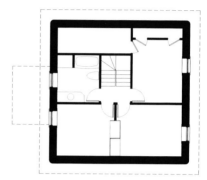

TOP: Main street elevation, Kanata 2000. ABOVE: Ground and first floor plans of demonstration house, Kahnawake.

The sites are oriented and planted for winter passive solar gain, summer shade, and wind breaks. Third, natural features and accessible common land with enhancements conducive to social gathering are preserved. Planting and grading are designed for technical, social, ecological, and economic benefits. Sites are minimally cleared and regraded using sustainable indigenous landscaping including edible plants and no-maintenance ground cover. Finally, an innovative water supply and treatment system based on grouped deep well supply is used. While addressing water quality problems, the system also provides the water volume necessary for firefighting through hydrant connections and both a natural habitat and aesthetically pleasing focus for the community space. Culverts are eliminated and site run-off is managed through planted swales.

THE DEMONSTRATION HOME

The demonstration house was not designed for a specific client. While there was a waiting list of potential homeowners, many of the community members most interested in housing alternatives were not themselves eligible under the existing housing allocation system. The Mohawk team members expressed a strong desire to make the demonstration project a model home for publicity's sake, rather than allow it to be immediately occupied. This approach ultimately prevailed, although we did, for a brief time, have a specific client—a single mother who was ready to engage in the process with her family's help before project delays as well as personal trepidation regarding the innovative nature of the house led her to withdraw her support. Design choices were therefore made by the housing and environment offices coordinators, and in the end, it was team member Lynn Jacobs who took the project on personally, engaging her family's and friends' help, and devoting long volunteer hours to its construction. Since the house's completion in June 2001, she has occupied it as her home and project office, monitoring its energy performance and giving tours as required.

The sweat equity program recognized the labor contribution and allowed for the budget to be increased. The $65,000 was allocated to include more sustainable materials, systems, and design strategies, and to ensure greater long-term affordability through reduced heating and repair costs. The house was designed as a slab on grade with a second, bedroom floor under the eaves and attic storage above. Other planning features include an ample vestibule, minimization of circulation space (replaced with habitable rooms), and an enclosed flexible ground floor room with adjacent bath. The house is also sited and fenestrated for maximum winter solar gain as well as for views of the rising and setting sun. Materials and systems include in-fill strawbale construction with a two-by-four balloon frame and lime stucco finish inside and out, an earth-block interior wall for additional thermal mass, galvalum roofing, radiant floor heating, and solar hot water system.

Strawbale was chosen not only for its material properties (R-40 insulation value, two hours' fire resistance, etc.) and affordability, but, perhaps more importantly, for its conviviality, as an easily understood and simply installed building product conducive to family participation. My own strawbale house in downtown Montreal, completed during the project's development, provided a tangible example for both the team and interested community members. In the spirit of a traditional barn-raising, the installation of the bales generated a wealth of good spirit and community cooperation. Participation in fact extended beyond Kahnawake's borders, and the material's novelty continues to attract attention today. Hands-on workshops in

Installation of strawbales by community members.

both strawbale installation and compressed earth-block fabrication brought out a few potential homeowners, as well as some interested local contractors who ultimately joined the construction team. Materials and systems were selected in part to enhance the skills of local workers and to generate new employment possibilities.

The demonstration project has proved a success on many levels. It remains to be seen who the ultimate occupants of the neighborhood will be and whether or not the housing and neighborhood form will provide a comfortable fit. The master plan may in fact require significant modification in order to be completed. Upon the completion of the demonstration home Kanata 2000's grassroots effort finally received the Band Council's full support.

REVIEWING RESULTS

Although there is still a long way to go in engaging the community at large, as well as securing additional funding for ongoing research, the construction of a sustainable, affordable demonstration home provides a tangible point of departure for future discussion, and much inspiration can be drawn from the students' participation and hundreds of volunteer hours from the project professionals and community members and leaders. In retrospect, none of the team members, including myself, was adequately trained to properly engage the community in the

Kanata 2000 project. Subsequent discussions with social scientists have given us new insight, tools, and prospects for collaboration that could result in greater outreach.

Our team had no idea, at the outset of this project, how layered and complex the process we were embarking on would prove. We were bolstered by a common vision of sustainability that carried us naively through innumerable obstacles. The project revealed how multi-dimensional and enriching minimum-cost housing and community development truly are. The process extends well beyond the traditional confines of an architect's professional services. As our work has shown, successful design efforts must go beyond standard material, technical, and programmatic criteria to include a thorough investigation of urban, cultural, social, psychological, political, and financial concerns. In our case, we identified many of the key issues on an ad hoc basis. Additional experience and further study will undoubtedly formalize new methodologies and better prepare architects and clients alike for the rewarding challenge of community design.

As generalists trained to synthesize multiple constraints into a coherent whole, architects have the unique potential to direct housing trends toward more sustainable community development. Minimum-cost housing has traditionally provided a fertile ground for architectural innovation as well as social commitment; yet we must work hard and fast to reclaim and redefine our legitimate role in the face of a disastrous recent history of simplistic large-scale projects, a conservative, recession-cautious housing industry, and a competitive market of building, planning, urban design, engineering, and interior design specialists. Ironically, we are being squeezed out of the housing industry at the same time that we are recognizing its desperate need for more care and professional attention.

The process is undeniably very costly in terms of an investment of professional time. Standard fee structures do not compensate for this kind of service, nor do minimum-cost housing or municipal planning budgets permit extensive investigations. Grants and subsidies are the mainstay of such efforts, but are generally too small, time-consuming to obtain, and burdened by administrative requirements. Universities clearly have a significant role to play in research and analysis, but may be out-of-touch with regard to current technologies, cost factors, and building practices. Students in particular generally lack the technical and costing expertise necessary to solve minimum-cost housing problems in a studio context, and the academic schedule puts constraints on construction efforts and long-term planning. Furthermore, First Nations communities in particular are discouraged, if not bitter, regarding universities' previous record of repeatedly "poking and prodding" and then disappearing with few concrete results and barely a written record.

New models that nurture the interdependence of academia, practice, industry, and community to direct and apply research must be developed. We must reassess both the products and the process in a much larger sense. We must move beyond our fixation with the preciousness of the object to develop our skills as mediators and offer our talents as synthetic thinkers adept at shifting from small details to large pictures and from poetic and mundane human concerns to technical and financial ones. The profession itself stands to be redefined and strengthened as a result. "What goes around, comes around," as they say; in reaching out, we may ourselves be legitimated.

HOMEOWNERSHIP FOR LOW-INCOME HOUSEHOLDS IN PUBLIC HOUSING

CHARLES HOCH AND TRACY LANIER

Homeownership is professed by many as the solution to economic and social problems. This study suggests that it might not be such a simple answer: real design solutions must consider complex layers of social factors.

CHARLES HOCH directs the Urban Planning and Policy Program at the University of Illinois at Chicago, where he teaches courses on planning theory, physical planning, and housing. His most recent housing publication is "Sheltering the Homeless in the US: Social Improvement and the Continuum of Care" in *Housing Studies*, 15:6 (2000): 865–76.

TRACY LANIER has worked extensively in social services with the homeless and mentally ill. She is committed to the use of affordable and supportive housing as a rehabilitation tool.

The social rationale for home ownership includes strong claims about the efficacy of ownership. The deep attachment to this belief led policymakers to believe that once low-income families obtained ownership, the families would experience social and economic improvements. Proponents like former U.S. Department of Housing and Urban Development (HUD) Secretary Jack Kemp argued that owning a home would empower renter households. The new owners, by conducting the responsibilities of ownership, would learn to act more autonomously. They would not only find the means to improve their own economic destiny, but improve their neighborhood as well. Linking ownership and household independence offers a powerful rhetorical claim for a popular housing tenure. But the evidence supporting the claim remains mixed. Poor people enjoy few resources to use when illness, death, unemployment, child-care difficulties or other unexpected but important social and family problems occur. Claiming that change in housing tenure will remedy longstanding social privations, economic disadvantages, and other aspects of poverty seems especially optimistic.

When households rent they consume housing but do not control its economic destiny. When households own they not only consume housing but manage and control its use as an investment good. This management requires knowledge, skills, and in many cases social attributes that low-income people who have never owned a house lack. Helping very poor people purchase and care for a home requires an elaborate scaffolding of support—a scaffolding often no better than its weakest link.

Historically federal government ownership programs like Section 235 of the 1968 Housing Act treated access to housing ownership as if low-income households possessed the knowledge necessary to manage an investment. Additionally, such programs were relatively insensitive to the location of dwellings. Dwellings were often concentrated in neighborhoods in a fashion that accelerated disinvestment. The poorly prepared new homeowners frequently failed to properly budget and care for their housing. The foreclosure rate accelerated depressing prospects for improved economic value nearby. Instead of enhancing neighborhoods, the programs became an engine of neighborhood decline.

SELF SUFFICIENCY

The self-sufficiency programs designed decades later expected recipient families to improve their economic autonomy and security. The federal self-sufficiency scheme begun in 1997 offered rent subsidies to program participants who agreed to participate in education, job training, and employment programs. However, few reached a level of economic and social autonomy independent of any form of public assistance. Six percent of the initial participants successfully graduated the five-year program.

State institutions also offered poor results. The Gateway Program in Charlotte, North Carolina, required adherence to an educational program in return for financial benefits. Analysts William A. Rohe and Rachel G. Kleit compared the program graduates with others who did not participate in the program as well as to those who dropped out.[1] The program did yield positive results for those who graduated, but those who withdrew did not in the end show less dependence than those who had never participated. As poor people receive education, job experience, and social support over several years we expect (even if they do not complete the course) that they would find work, improve their earnings, reduce reliance on

[1] William A. Rohe and Rachel G. Kleit, *Gateway Housing Program Report to Congress* (Washington, D.C.: Office of Policy Development and Research, HUD, March 1997).

aid, and rent housing in the conventional housing market more frequently than those who did not participate at all. But they did not.

The people who designed the Gateway Program imagined households with few problems, but in fact the problems were many. Only one caseworker was assigned to manage the one hundred households in the program, including very poor and vulnerable participants. All but a few percent were headed by single females with children. Ninety percent had children twelve years old and younger, while 86% received less than $1,000 income a month. Family responsibilities, mainly child-care, undermined efforts to maintain schooling. It seems that people's motivation to participate in the program reflected their interest in obtaining a public housing unit as much as participating in a self-sufficiency program. Hence, the lackluster participation in program requirements may have been the product of the initial selection process. The program officers presumed a level of preparation and commitment among public housing residents that did not exist. Additionally relocation into program housing resulted in participants being isolated from supportive friends and neighbors.

MIXED-INCOME COMMUNITY

In 1990, Congress began creating a series of programs loosely associated by the title "Homeownership and Opportunity for People Everywhere" (HOPE). The last in this series of HOPE programs is HOPE VI, created in 1990 to revitalize severely distressed or obsolete public housing developments. This program, administered by HUD, attempts to remedy the worst elements of large, high-density public housing. HOPE VI relies on implementing improvements to the existing projects that will produce a mixed-income community. If the problem of the projects is the super concentration of very poor people, then the solution requires breaking up such local concentrations. The improved communities need to attract a more economically diversified clientele, including homeowners. The strategies thus call for a mix of rental and homeowner housing for a range of income groups—including ownership for eligible public housing residents.

One of the earliest programs putting HOPE VI to use was Earle Village in Charlotte, North Carolina. This case bears special importance because the effort combined the beliefs in the efficacy of ownership with the policy shift to move people away from reliance on public assistance and improve household self-reliance.[2]

2 Holly Grosvenor, "Earle Village, A Community in Transition," *Urban Land* (January 1996): 50–54.

3 Linda B. Fosberg, Susan J. Popkin, and Gretchen Lake, *An Historical Baseline Assessment of HOPE VI, Volume I Gross Site Review* (Washington, D.C.: Department of Housing and Urban Development, July 1996).

Constructed in downtown Charlotte in 1967, Earle Village public housing included 400 new apartments that replaced less than a third of the 1500 dwellings torn down. Similar to projects in Chicago and other large cities, Earle Village ended up fostering social dependence and stigma among very poor neighbors. However, in comparison to other troubled public housing projects, almost thirty years later Earle Village was only one of two that received a good physical condition rating. In fact, Earle Village had better management and fewer problems with property destruction and gangs than most other troubled projects evaluated by HUD.[3] Ironically, a 1994 plan for Earle Village further reduced the number of subsidized units. The project plans included a community plaza, daycare facility, a community service center, and, most prominently, seventy-five town homes slated for homeownership by local residents. The plan also included 170

The demolition of Stateway Public Housing in 2002 erases a community and reflects a change in HUD strategy from rental to home ownership.

transitional or family self-sufficiency units and 68 rental units for the elderly.[4] Household social improvement was a crucial rationale. Low-income households were supposed to filter up through the project. The poorest would live initially in the newly named transitional units and participate in the family self-sufficiency programs, moving from welfare to work.

[4] Carol D. Leonnig, "Success with Bricks, but not with Earle Village's People," *News and Observer*, 14 June 1999.

Despite the upbeat rhetoric of the Earle Village project, ownership by public housing residents proved too difficult. People with annual incomes as low as $5000 were not likely in five years to find employment that paid enough to make the monthly payments for town homes priced at $95,000. Participants did not move up the ladder of social improvement at Earle Village.

Economically, building a residential community with dwellings and amenities sufficiently attractive to draw middle-income residents required improvements to local infrastructure and facilities that in turn would raise property values and land prices nearby. Socially, middle-income buyers expect that most of their neighbors will be of similar or higher social standing. So attracting such buyers to a mixed-income community requires that the proportion of low-income households is small, perhaps as low as 5 or 10%. Since most HOPE VI developments reduce the density of the earlier public housing projects, the mixed-income strategy necessarily requires dispersing most of the poor residents to other locations. In Earle Village, the housing authority did not build additional offsite public housing to make up for what was lost. As of June 1999 only about 5% of the poor families displaced appeared willing and able to enter the mixed-income community.[5]

[5] Ibid.

Efforts linking household improvement and ownership as currently constructed will likely produce high drop-out rates. It seems more reasonable to presume that ownership requires social and economic prerequisites that few single-parent households can obtain or produce on their own. These households need support from others. But such support need not be described as dependency.

It might prove better to distinguish participation in household improvement and home-ownership programs. Instead of envisioning ownership as a kind of tool for household empowerment, it would be better to conceive of it in terms of multiple types of housing security arrayed along a continuum from exclusive ownership at one end to shared owner-ship at the other. Design ownership programs should offer participants with relatively low levels of economic and social strength a wider choice of ownership participation options. We next review two program options that attempt to do just this.

LEASE TO OWN

The lease-to-own model uses institutional resources to help low-income households cross the threshold of social and economic independence needed to make ownership a benefi-cial tenure. These programs acknowledge that most low-income homeowners need time and assistance to build financial strength, increase incomes, and learn to manage and care for their own dwelling. Lease-to-own programs not only provide subsidies but work with individual households to prepare them to assume the responsibilities of ownership.

Economically, the lease-to-own strategy postpones purchase of a home and uses its initial stage to support household improvement efforts. The promise of ownership helps motivate and ultimately reward such efforts. This strategy helps poor resident households to move consistently toward economic self-reliance. Households learn not only to improve their employment prospects in local labor markets, but also how to manage the responsibilities of housing ownership. National research suggests that such changes are difficult to accom-plish for those in the middle ranks of the public-housing population. The programs tend to cream off those already doing well among their peers.

One well-established lease-to-own model involves seller-financed land-installment con-tracts. Here low-income residents purchase the dwelling they inhabit from the owner, who finances the purchase for the resident. Nonprofit organizations have adopted this model in order to increase access to ownership among households unable to obtain conventional financing. The nonprofit institutes a fixed lease period during which time the lease holder establishes (or improves) credit, increases income, takes responsibility for the care of the dwelling, creates and balances a household budget, pays down the debt through monthly payments, and saves income. In effect, the lease arrangement serves as a kind of home-owner apprenticeship.

In Chicago the Logan Square Neighborhood Association (LSNA) collaborates with the local housing authority to help public housing residents purchase homes. In 1999 LSNA obtained eleven properties appraised between $90,000 and $99,000 for a lease-to-own program. Additionally LSNA provides homeownership training, which includes education

Hundreds of low-income rental units are demolished under the new HUD policy.

about the relative advantages of buying versus renting a dwelling. LSNA contracts with a local religious organization for case management services to cope with household vulnerabilities. It offers training on property maintenance, home decorating, landscaping, and gardening. Potential owners learn about fire safety and code enforcement and receive advice about energy and water conservation to keep utility costs down. Additional help is offered on property insurance, record keeping, budgeting, and receiving tax benefits.

LSNA did not foresee some of the challenges of their program. Residents are reluctant to adopt new tasks like snow removal, leaf raking, and other seasonal chores. Requiring mandatory attendance at the monthly homeowner meetings has fostered resentments. Administrative foot dragging over approving financing packages undermines the promise of ownership for participants. In the meantime, residents attend homeownership training, access the case manager, use educational referrals, and not so patiently await the inception of the lease-holding phase.

COOPERATIVES

Another viable model for low-income homeownership is the cooperative, whose structure provides an institutional framework for sharing the burdens and benefits of ownership. The cooperative pools the economic resources of strangers and seeks to build residential community through a series of shared activities and agreements. Residents of a limited equity cooperative purchase shares of a building upon becoming members, and the shares entitle each to possession of a dwelling. But no member enjoys exclusive claim to a specific dwelling, nor do individual members sell the dwelling they inhabit. Members may sell their shares when they leave the cooperative.

Individual owners do not control their dwelling as an investment, but as a consumer good. The collective arrangements limit the equity of the participants. When households move out they do not receive more equity than they paid in. This approach enables the coop to remain affordable, especially in neighborhoods with increasing property values, precisely because members agree not to sell their shares at local market rates. Bickerdike, a Community Development Corporation in Chicago, organizes limited equity cooperatives because they become islands of affordability in appreciating local real-estate markets.

The cooperative structure enables low-income members to reduce housing costs, retain possession of their dwelling, and build equity—benefits that renters do not enjoy. Although the financial costs are lower, the social costs are higher in cooperatives, as participants must become active members of the residential community. There are also organizational costs: the formation of a cooperative or mutual housing association requires the knowledge and support of intermediary institutions to form and establish a collective ownership agreement. It takes time to educate and persuade folks about the merits of the cooperative's governing structure, shared ownership arrangements, and limited equity features.

In a case study in Nashville, Tennessee, initial activities included intensive weekend meetings to foster social ties, nurture indigenous leadership, and practice management skills. As the project progressed members received individual tutorials on household repairs including tools and manuals. Elected members participated in training to inform effective self-government, physical management, budget development, and selection of future members. This well-planned and expensive training enabled a cooperative, operated by residents with an average income of $14,008, to gain full independence in only three years. [6]

Obstacles to successful cooperatives flow less from individual households than from institutional impediments imposed by funders, regulating agencies, and other actors in local real estate. Financial and government institutions often resist or oppose efforts to build cooperatives.

[6] **William A. Rohe and Michael A. Stegman, "Converting Public Housing to Cooperatives: The Experience of Three Developments,"** *Housing Policy Debate* **6:2 (1995): 439–79.**

CONCLUSION

The relationship between social improvement policy and ownership policy should be carefully distinguished. While for some households the responsibilities of ownership might improve economic and social autonomy, others with similar family composition and income might experience these responsibilities as a burden too difficult to carry. Instead of designing and evaluating ownership programs as a means of household autonomy, the programs might better identify kinds and levels of household independence that improve prospects for successful ownership.

Studies of self-sufficiency found few poor single-parent households achieving the kinds and amount of independence defined in programs' goals. Households did enjoy better housing and show evidence of improved autonomy using improved social and economic support, but what most were able to achieve fell short. This may be because the programs did not work properly (for instance, many lacked sustained social support). It also may mean that the goals are too ambitious.

With the community dispersed, the previous residents will have no input into the goals or design of the new housing.

The design of such programs imagines households moving through a system as independent social units. This overlooks the network of interdependencies that shape single-parent families. High drop-out rates flow in large part from disruptive social demands such as a sick child, domestic abuse, or economic privations.[7] Participants need the help of other participants to meet routine social demands among family members and mutual encouragement from others struggling to do what it takes to keep working and handle ownership tasks. Social reciprocity among participants, if properly encouraged, can become a shared asset. But living together for a long period of time works against a household improvement strategy that focuses on the upward mobility of individual families.

The recently designed and currently implemented Jobs-Plus welfare-to-work program sponsored by HUD seeks to use the social and community ties among residents to build support for working among program participants. In Chicago, Lakefront SRO has adopted a strong, supportive housing program that includes an employment placement and counseling program that combines staff efforts with the community support gained from shared residential living.[8]

[7] Rohe and Kleit emphasize the importance of social solidarity and mutual support among a cohort of program participants. Rohe and Kleit, *Gateway Housing*, 75–86.

[8] Jean Butzen, "Lakefront SRO Corporation: Reviving Single Room Occupancy Housing," in George Hemmens, Charles Hoch, and Jana Carp, eds., *Under One Roof: Issues and Innovations in Shared Housing* (Albany, NY: SUNY Press, 1996), 75–86.

A balanced program design would include options that allow individual households to improve rapidly toward autonomy, while also paying attention to the progress of cohorts. This means developing forms of shared housing that provide a combination of temporary and permanent housing for participants. The programs should include different levels along a continuum from dependence to independence. The lease-to-own program stretches the continuum, but does not offer viable alternatives besides owning or renting. Cooperatives sacrifice long-term wealth development for low-cost entry and security of possession. Owning a share with limited equity controls does not provide the kind of social autonomy and economic accumulation at the center of the homeownership dream.

The results of this review suggest that public efforts to support and subsidize ownership for low-income public housing residents may be ill advised. The resources currently channeled to meet the hopes of policymakers might be better spent providing programs and assistance that better fit the expectations and means of the poor themselves. Public investments that build the social solidarity and organizational strength of viable but troubled neighborhoods may prove more beneficial than targeting weak individual households.

ARCHITECTURE AS ARTIFACT: HOUSING FOR MIGRANT FARMWORKERS
BRYAN BELL

The following essay illustrates research and a participatory design process conducted to understand and respond to the specific needs of housing for migrant farmworkers in one Pennsylvania county.

BRYAN BELL is the director of Design Corps, a nonprofit architecture firm based in Raleigh, North Carolina, that he founded in 1991. He has taught community design-build at three architecture schools, including twelve projects at the Auburn Rural Studio. In 1995, Bell started the Design Corps Fellowship program, which allows recent graduates to design for the underserved.

"All architectural practice must be preceded by intense field study among the people for whom the architect plans to build, from whom he [or she] has stolen the right to design."
—Henry Glassie[1]

[1] Henry Glassie in Clement Greenburg, editor, *Art and Culture: Critical Essays* (Boston: Beacon Press, 1961), 61.

One effective way to evaluate how well a building responds to its users is to view the result as an archeologist views an artifact from the ancient past. The more the archeologist can learn about the past from an object, the closer the object is related to the culture that produced it. Similarly, the better a building accommodates the many specifics of an individual, a family, or a community, the better it is as an artifact.

The architect, unlike the archeologist, creates the object, rather than reading from an object that already exists. Architects are the designers, the form-givers. This is our skill. We can give two-dimensional vision and three-dimensional reality to the needs and dreams of individuals and communities. Every form we use is packed with cultural values and social implications—the "content." If we assume the role of form-maker for others, we have a great responsibility to understand the cultural identity of the client so that the object responds to the

Migrant farmworker in Pennsylvania.

client's identity, not to our own. This understanding can be difficult to achieve, especially if the client and designer are from different backgrounds. Since many designers come from a small cultural pool of education, income, race and ethnicity, serving the greater public requires that we first understand the backgrounds of each client.

As designers, we tend to focus on creating beautiful forms but often overlook the social implications of what we create. Failing to simultaneously create the forms and consider their content is to subconsciously create forms with meanings that we do not understand, or forms more appropriate for ourselves than for the forms' users.

A productive design process constantly cross-pollinates between form and content. Just as we work between sketches and models in designing, working between form and content provides different information about the same thing. The dialog between the two enriches the process and ignites fresh design ideas. Articulating a specific individual's or community's values and living patterns should be the goal of any architectural design.

[2] The work was funded by grants from the American Institute of Architects/American Architectural Foundation and the National Endowment for the Arts, two sources that supported the extended community-based process involved.

The following project illustrates one effort to understand the issues and needs of a specific group, categorized by their common labor practice as migrant farmworkers, and their relationship to the housing and culture they enter as traveling labor.[2] Only after researching the precedents of migrant housing in Adams County, Pennsylvania—the farmers who built it and the workers who lived in it—and including migrants in the design of their homes, was I able to make form from content.

THE RESEARCH PHASE

The development of housing specifically for migrant farmworkers is a recent occurrence, emerging after World War II when farms shifted their labor source from local residents to out-of-state workers. The new workers were families from the southern United States, both black and white. They were the first large group to travel between states to harvest, and the

Housing for a migrant family, section and floor plan.

first to need short-term housing. This housing was largely hit-or-miss; created without design analysis, good ideas were often not shared while bad ones were repeated. The easiest solution was to relocate small existing buildings, moving them to the farms. Typically, these first units consisted of one room without plumbing. Many of these cabins are still used for migrant housing around Adams County, Pennsylvania, today.

In the early 1960s, single workers, also from the South, replaced the families. For this new labor force, a new type of housing evolved: the dormitory, with its infamous variant, the "bullpen," so called because many single men bunk in one large room. Bullpens have proved to be one of the worst designs for the workers that come to central Pennsylvania to pick apples, cherries, and peaches.

In the 1970s, there were changes in the demographics of the farm communities in Adams County. Men from Puerto Rico, then Jamaica, then Haiti and Mexico began to show up looking for work. In some years, many cultures mixed together in tight quarters, and this led to conflicts.

The design of the dormitory housing caused several problems. Since there was only a single kitchen, food had to be prepared in bulk, cafeteria-style. It was difficult for the individual to assume an equal share of cleaning responsibilities; understandably, no single person would clean a bathroom that sixty people shared. These and similar problems required a central authority in the form of a crew leader—a labor contractor who dealt with local growers and recruited farmworkers—and his authority led to abuses in overcharging for food and services. It was difficult to stop such abuses without changing the type of housing as well.

In response to growing problems and the notoriety of migrant housing during the 1970s, many states became directly involved in monitoring and even in licensing migrant housing. In 1973, Pennsylvania passed the Migrant and Seasonal Farm Labor Act, a building code that was intended to prevent the most common sorts of abuse. For example, it defined a maximum number of people allowed to use one shower, one toilet, one stove. And for the first time, the size of the housing determined the number of workers that could occupy the camp: one hundred square feet for each adult and fifty square feet for each child.

These laws led to sweeping improvements and a new type of farm worker housing; the motel style, also known as the "horse stall" to migrants, were side-by-side sleeping rooms, usually for four persons. Each room had a stove, sink, and refrigerator, but bathrooms were still communal. An occupant had to exit his room to the outside and walk down the row of rooms, usually to one end, to access the bathroom.

THE PARTICIPATORY DESIGN PHASE

We at Design Corps decided to help make migrant housing better, as growers will continue to need to house single adult males of many cultures. We began by meeting with Rural Opportunities, Farmworker Advisory Council, and other farmworker groups in Pennsylvania to gain an understanding of our clients' needs. Sixty-three percent of workers surveyed in Pennsylvania were from Mexico, followed by 17% from Puerto Rico, 8% from the United States, 7% from Haiti, and 5% from Jamaica. We then gathered less formal input from groups in New Jersey, New York, and Ohio. Since our target group was migratory, we wanted to see what they held in common with men from other areas, and what was unique to each area.

In response to the cultural diversity of migrants, we decided to build smaller detached buildings that could house groups from the same countries. We showed this as well as other design proposals to a small advisory group of both farmers and workers to gain their feedback. A manufactured unit presented some solutions, such as preapproval to housing regulations and pre-pricing, both of which would interest the growers. We designed a two-bedroom unit to start the group conversations. We decided that two bedrooms would better accommodate the families that had increased in number in the migrant stream after the 1986 Immigration Reform and Control Act. Although starting with a design before talking with workers was less than ideal, we found that the model and drawings were very effective in soliciting input from them. To elicit first responses to the model design, we handed out questionnaires in English and Spanish that addressed our main concerns, and then moved to a less prescriptive and informal conversation in which the workers' candid opinions emerged.

Workers generally liked our design for its consideration of needs such as a tool storage closet and an accessible wash area for pesticide cleanup. But the building's shed roof was not liked by some. Milton Cunningham, an African-American worker from Georgia, said the roof reminded him of a turkey shed. We altered the design in the next version to a low-pitched gable. The response to this second design was better, and so we built it.

At this point, we sought and received funds that would provide an incentive for the growers to build this better housing, which exceeded the minimal floor area by 75%. The Pennsylvania Department of Community and Economic Development granted funds that would be forgiven over twenty years if the grower complied with all the standards for maintenance and rents.

We built four units in 1995, and their post-occupancy reviews were high, both by the workers who lived in them and the grower who maintains them. Residents particularly liked the front porch. Puerto Ricans thought its design to be Puerto Rican-style, while Mexicans liked to use it after work. So far, only single males, not families, have occupied the units, though we had planned for families to use the detached units if needed. The older types of migrant housing were particularly bad at housing families, and, since the 1986 Immigration and Reform Act, many families were traveling in the migrant labor stream and having a very difficult time with housing.

Workers provided some suggestions to better the design, such as the addition of a cabinet for the garbage can. This comment showed that they had pride in the housing, which we expected to increase by decreasing the numbers of residents per unit. Similarly, several men said the light-colored floors were hard to keep clean, especially the first year when there was no grass on the site and dirt was easily tracked inside. We observed that each unit put its one television in one of the bedrooms, rather than in the communal dining area. The men from the other room had to come and sit on the floor to watch it.

Based on the comments and observations of the first unit's field test, we took a different approach in the second round of design and building. We designed a specific unit for single workers and another for a family. These two main groups were very different, and creating two designs allowed for a more specific response. The more that was learned about migrant culture, the better we could accommodate their needs and values. The more specific our understanding became, the more specific our design could become.

The single workers told us they did not want to stay in Pennsylvania, in contrast to the assumption made by most local residents. They came for the money and then wanted to go home. The unit we designed for them expressed this mobility as a horizontal vehicle, with only minimal attachment to the earth. The design does not favor one culture over

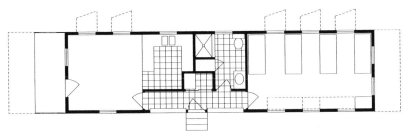

Migrant housing for single males, roadside view, floor plan, and study model. The unit was manufactured off-site and set up by a crane.

another, as the occupants vary from year to year, but it does express the value they have in common: mobility. The new unit has one bedroom for four men, with a table for the television that all can see from their beds.

In contrast, the families traveling together sought permanence, particularly for the sake of their children's education. Therefore, the unit designed for them, who are still in the migrant stream but desire to settle out of it, expressed stability and a strong attachment to the ground. The exterior is made of solid masonry-like products called Hardi-plank and Hardi-panel. To anchor the unit to the site, the vertical is emphasized in a continuous foundation wall and porch. We designed the unit to be built in modules. It has two bedrooms on two floors, and its two units are stacked in a "double-high" coupling (as opposed to a double-wide). When this design was shown to farm workers, their most common response was that it looked "like a temple." Others said it looked like three apple trees. We felt our expression of their Mexican (Mayan) culture and their work context was successful, that in this way it had become an artifact for those who would live in it.

The houses for the single workers were built and occupied for the first harvest season in 2002, and the residents have offered very positive responses during visits by the designers. Future discussions during a three-year period of assessment will tell more as a greater number of residents evaluate the design.

As the concept of participatory design shows, architects can, if they view their creative act as making artifacts for others, effectively provide for the design needs of the diverse public. This approach allows for designers to respond equally successfully to all, dispelling the notion that good design is only about high incomes and high construction costs. Good design is about careful consideration of the individual.

LIGHT
JAE CHA

Nonprofit organizations are officially designated and recognized as being "for the good of the public." Many nonprofits build projects such as low-income housing but do not include creating quality designs as part of their mission. A nonprofit that provides architectural services, such as Light, has the clear mission to accomplish both.

JAE CHA received her M.Architecture from Yale University School of Architecture in 1999 and founded Light, a nonprofit corporation, in 2000. She has received two Research and Design Awards for her work in South and Central America.

It was unbearably hot in Marcovia, Honduras. During my summers in the United States, I drove and worked in air-conditioned cars and buildings. I only felt the heat if I chose to, when I walked to and from my car to these places. In Marcovia, where there was no electricity or running water, the only choice was to feel the heat during the day and the humidity brought about by tropical rains in the evenings. I worked in this environment one recent summer among 2,500 families, whose original homes and lives were destroyed by a hurricane.

In Marcovia, with the exception of a local food store and a small school, public space in which people can freely congregate, away from the heat and humidity, does not exist. Until now, public gatherings were held only in the evenings, when it was cooler, in an open field lit with gas lanterns. We proposed a new community center and church that could function during the day; it would contain public activities such as basic training and skill classes in addition to holding worship services. Planning and design took six months in the United States; I oversaw the construction on site over three months and completed the project in September 2001 with many people who volunteered their time, energy, and resources.

FIRST PROJECTS

My relationship with developing communities began when my family moved to Washington, D.C., from Korea in 1983. We became part of a Protestant church, which during my absence to study architecture began to support Christian mission and humanitarian projects. One elder of the church said to me upon my return, "You have been given so much; why don't you now use your architectural training for people in developing countries?" He was in the medical profession and had used his skills to provide services in those communities. His own life reflected his advice, which left a lasting impression on me.

Architecture was my passion, but it did not answer the larger questions about the meaning of life and why I should continue to pursue design. If architecture was indeed to be my life's journey and profession, I wanted it to have a purpose that would satisfy a cause beyond my own daily needs, motivated by my own faith and love for God. The elder continued to challenge me and suggested that I visit Bolivia on a volunteer mission trip that summer. When I returned, he asked me if I could design a small worship space for Urubo, Bolivia, a small village of 150 families, which had a small congregation of Christians but was in need of a worship space.

It was at this time that the first Architecture Research and Design Emerging Architecture Competition results, sponsored by London's *Architectural Review*, were published. The winner was d-line, a Norwegian architectural team that built an orphanage in Nepal. I was shocked and excited to see this project, because it exposed me to the possibilities of how architecture could be used for those in need and how I could integrate the elder's suggestions into my life. For the next year, as I continued to work on the church in Bolivia, I kept the orphanage photographs on my desk for inspiration and direction. The natural beauty of Nepal and its people, which was so artfully expressed through the photographs, moved me.

As I started to design the church in Bolivia, I wanted to express the Spirit that would move others as they experienced the building. I looked toward the verse, "Now the Lord is the Spirit, and where the Spirit of the Lord is, there is free-dom."[1] This became the concept for the church. The result was a design for 150 people that was circular in plan, equally open to all sides, permitting anyone, regardless of their background, lifestyle, or attitudes, to observe or participate freely in

[1] 2 Corinthians 3:16.

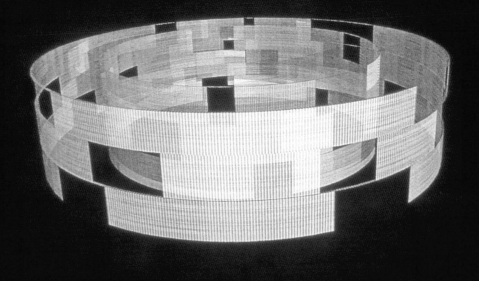

Conceptual model expressing, "Where the Spirit of the Lord is, there is freedom."

worship. The open plan allowed for people to sit on individual stools and move about as they wished, unlike the prescribed, fixed way dictated by pews in conventional church design. I wanted to convey that as believers in Jesus Christ, laws do not bind us, but that through grace, we are called to be free—in love, not condemnation.

The design process took eight months, during which I communicated with a local pastor working in Urubo via fax and e-mail to send and receive drawings and photos. Although I had visited Bolivia, through him I was able to gain a deeper understanding for the needs of the community, address construction and material limitations, and develop a sensitivity for the site. The project evolved into one specifically for women and children because, with little local economy, men worked in remote cities for weeks at a time and women were left to take care of the home. The church was completed in August 2000, in ten days, with many volunteers both local and from the United States.

NEW CHALLENGES

As I reflect on both the Honduras and Bolivia projects, I realize that they were results of the pure joy I felt while working with these communities, and not selfless acts. I am thankful for the many people whose support through material donations—under Light, a nongovernmental, nonprofit organization—made it possible to fund the projects. With goals to provide small-scale civic architecture in developing areas to foster community empowerment and vitality, Light is dedicated to creating public spaces that provide the physical foundation for economically diverse, self-supported, and self-guided communities.

TOP: The church was built in ten days. ABOVE: Interior view of church/community center in Urubo, Bolivia.

plan
0   2m

elevation
0   2m

LEFT: A view of the corridor shows patterns of light and shadow. TOP RIGHT: An open plan allows for people to move about as they wish. LOWER RIGHT: Elevation showing the wall pattern.

But as in any new practice, it was difficult at times, and I did many odd jobs to keep the vision going. No matter how difficult the process, I was determined to continue because of the memories of the people that shaped my life. I remember one incident when I became ill in Marcovia. After my recovery, local people gave me a large plate of mangos and watermelons. I was so moved by this gesture because food was scarce and had to be rationed during my entire stay. At that moment, I was overwhelmed with thankfulness as I realized how I often overlooked all the blessings in my life, in the same way I overlooked the fruits that were so common and abundant back home.

Although the needs in developing communities are great and architecture alone cannot solve all their problems, design is part of a larger good working toward economic sustainability. Without architecture, vaccinations cannot be provided, people cannot be educated, and the public cannot assemble; places such as Marcovia and Urubo need environments to facilitate these activities to prevent disease, provide education, and allow for collective activities.[2] In this light, maximizing the usage of a building by planning a multipurpose, open public space is important. What is at once a church could, at another time, serve as a community center or as classrooms.

[2] Conversation with John Riker, New York, 2001.

For architecture to be significant in a developing community, it needs to be responsive and responsible to local conditions and climate, capitalizing on existing resources for a community that is already in need. Partnering with local skilled labor to produce efficient build-

TOP: Local Bolivian and American volunteers in a circle. ABOVE: Night view.

sources (natural light and ventilation, photovoltaics) can reduce long-term maintenance costs and extend the usage of the building. Remote areas, where it is impossible to hold programs related to health care and education due to the lack of electricity, can benefit greatly from these nondependent technologies.[3]

I am currently working on a project in a developing community in Costa Rica. Similar to the Bolivia and Honduras projects, this will help to lift the myth that development work is uninspired, engineering-led, or has to follow the local vernacular style.[4] I want to continue designing based on *Light Construction*[5] attitudes toward construction; *Touch the Earth Lightly*[6] attitudes toward sustainable architecture; and *Lightness*[7] attitudes toward minimum structures. In this way, minimal resources can be maximized for substantial impact for these communities.

Eventually, I would like to collaborate with others, and if the opportunity to design more conventional expensive buildings arises, I will take on that challenge. But for the moment, my efforts will be to continue with Light. This is because I have tasted that "light is sweet."[8]

[3] Conversation with Anna Dyson, New York, 2001.

[4] Conversation with Conrad James, London, 2001.

[5] Terence Riley, *Light Construction* (New York: Museum of Modern Art, 1995).

[6] Philip Drew and Glen Murcutt, *Touch the Earth Lightly* (Australia: Duffy & Snellgrove, 1996).

[7] Adrian Beukers and Ed van Hinte, *Lightness* (Rotterdam: 010 Publishers, 2001).

[8] Ecclesiastes 11:7.

SIX-SQUARE HOUSE
KIM NEUSCHELER

In Project Row Houses, a neighborhood social service agency acts as an intermediary between the community and a design-build program, directing their efforts into well-understood directions. Though the eventual house occupants are not involved in the decision making, the local nonprofit has a sophisticated understanding of design and the benefits it can provide for a community.

Upon conclusion of the architecture program at Rice University, KIM NEUSCHELER remained in Houston to work on the Rice Building Workshop House until its completion in 1999. She is currently working for a New York construction company on a new research laboratory.

Nestled between rickety old homes and a community in need of serious restoration lies a creative environment dedicated to historic preservation, community service, and youth education. This unique development, known as Project Row Houses, is a nonprofit organization established to revitalize a partially abandoned Houston Third Ward neighborhood rich in African-American history and culture. The natural cadence established by rows of similar shotgun homes compels the visitor to look a little more closely at the subtle differences that give this place its charming character. Small deviations in design elements from one house to the next, from door and window details to trim styles and colors, leave observers wondering just what they have not seen. And should visitors spend an afternoon wandering around, discovering all the simple beauties of this place, they are bound to witness a community come to life as students start returning from school and parents from a hard day at work to participate in the bustling activity that is synonymous with Project Row Houses—an activity that has consumed the lives of Rice Building Workshop students for several years.

THE DESIGN-BUILD STUDIO

The Rice Building Workshop was created to give students hands-on, practical experience with real-life projects within the Houston community. The project types vary in subject matter and size and offer the students an opportunity to explore innovative solutions within the parameters set by the program. Most students walk away from this workshop with valuable knowledge in hand and a better understanding of the organization and level of commitment required to accomplish projects within and for a community.

One such project during my spring semester in the program was to design a low-cost house that would eventually become a part of Project Row Houses. After visiting the site and understanding the context within which this house was to be built, I and the other students of the Rice Building Workshop began our work. The building typology and vocabulary of the row houses were evident in the resounding wood siding, low-pitched metal roofs, double-hung windows, elevated foundations, and much-valued porch spaces. Our design process was almost intuitive given this existing language, which served as the governing design criteria for the new house. The director of Project Row Houses, Rick Lowe, requested that we respect the surrounding materials and building typology. He believed it was

These vernacular houses from Houston's Third Ward suggested the design language and "governing design criteria" for the new prototype design.

important that this house celebrate the characteristics that gave this neighborhood its distinct identity: simple materials, spaces to congregate, and subtle differences that encouraged individuality while seemingly conforming to the collective whole.

Eleven students were split into five teams to develop new ideas for the house. At the onset of the project, it was unclear as to which part of Project Row Houses this building would ultimately belong. It could be a residence for a single mother and her children, a studio and exhibition space for a local artist, or a building for part of the after-school programs for the neighborhood children. The only prerequisite provided was that the building be no more than nine hundred square feet. This lack of a definite program made design flexibility imperative and became a main concern for us students. We all wanted to provide an adaptable solution to accommodate any program and offer the opportunity

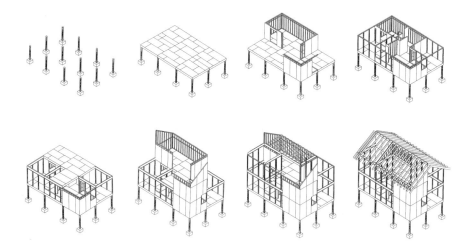

Diagram showing six-square module and construction phases.

to change that decision at any time. We had to think about the "what if" instead of the "must have." Specific clients bring with them particular ideas about program, so without this client input, we had to make certain assumptions about what our client might need or want.

Another important design issue was the location of the house on the site. The land selected for this project was a middle lot between residences for single mothers on the south side and sites for future dwellings on the north side. The class made a unanimous decision to locate the building on the easternmost side of the lot. This placement created an opportunity for a direct visual and physical relationship with the existing row houses to the south and east, while opening up views of downtown Houston to the north and west. The majority of our schemes were two-story structures that took advantage of these views and considered the probability that more houses would someday follow. This house was to be the prototype from which future houses would be modeled and provided an impetus for continued residential and community development.

CHOOSING A DESIGN

Throughout the semester, each team reviewed its scheme with the Rice Building Workshop directors, Danny Samuels and Nonya Grenader. They provided constructive criticism, insight, and incessant encouragement to further our designs. The teams also presented their schemes to the class and received helpful comments from their peers for the final stages of design development. Toward the end of the semester, two different design juries were held—one decided by the members of the class and the other composed of university professors, local architects, and the directors of Project Row Houses. Both juries unanimously selected the design by Katherine Dy and me. The selection of our design brought me an extended relationship with the Rice Building Workshop, Project Row Houses, and the community, a relationship that I will always treasure.

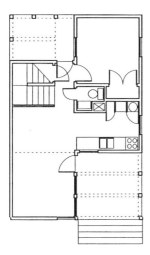
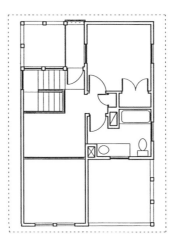

First and second floor plans clearly show the functions defined with the six-square modules.

Our scheme fulfilled the design criteria established by Project Row Houses and the Rice Building Workshop. The house would be constructed with indigenous materials and followed the building typology characteristic of the existing row houses. The design was simple and was defined by the local context. A single roof of corrugated metal covered this shotgun home and the porch spaces at each end. Its modular nature was seen as a design asset in that it created the potential for prefabrication of all or some of its parts and the probability for a shorter duration of construction. The house borrowed most of its vocabulary from the neighboring structures: pier and beam construction, double-hung windows for cross ventilation, wood siding, indoor/outdoor rooms, and views to its surroundings. It offered multiuse spaces as well as more defined rooms that provided the greatest possibility for future adaptation once a program was finalized. The clear flow of spaces minimized the need for superfluous circulation and maximized the efficiency of the plan.

The scheme was based on a six square module of ten-feet-eight-inch squares stacked on top of another six-square module. The composition was two squares wide by three squares deep, giving the overall footprint of the house a dimension of twenty-one feet four inches by thirty-two feet. The modular scheme could be reconfigured in a number of ways to accommodate a variety of programs for the house. Here the southeast and northwest corners were dedicated to double-height porches. On any given day, not a porch in the neighborhood sat lifeless while neighbors congregated to share life stories and ideas. For us, the porch was a very special place and merited celebration, hence the two-story space. The southeast porch connected to other Project Row Houses while the northwest porch related more closely with downtown Houston. The remaining squares within the house were essentially split down the middle. The more public rooms occupied the west-side squares and enjoyed double-height spaces, an abundance of light, and views of downtown. The more private rooms occupied the east-side squares; their single-height ceilings had a more personal scale and reflected back on the existing row houses.

DESIGN TO CONSTRUCTION

With the semester's end and my impending graduation, it was time to make a very important decision: return home to New York or remain in Houston, find a job, and see the house designed in the Rice Building Workshop through to its completion. I chose the latter and have not a single regret. It remains the most rewarding experience I have ever had and gave me a newly found passion for the profession in which I was about to embark. We spent that summer with construction documents and raising funds. We did most of this work in the evening and on weekends. In order to acquire community support, we prepared a fund-raising brochure to depict the workshop's goals and introduce the house to the public. The Rice Building Workshop and Project Row Houses met with various members of the community, corporations, foundations, and art organizations, all of whom offered monetary, material, and labor support. As the fall semester began, we had received enough donations and completed enough preparatory work to begin the home's construction.

When the fall arrived, a new semester of Rice Building Workshop students joined the project. The focus shifted from design to construction of the house. The students prepared the necessary shop drawings from which the house was built and refined outstanding design issues. The modular structure of the house allowed the floor and wall panels—constructed of two-by-four wood framing and half-inch plywood sheathing—to be prefabricated offsite in the civil engineering lab on Rice's campus. We staked the house out on the site, and completed the foundation work as the panel fabrication concluded. By simultaneously preparing these panels and the construction site we saved time with the initial framing.

I will never forget the day the wall and floor panels arrived at the site, stacked on the back of a truck. It was a cold, wet Saturday morning. It had been raining for a couple of days, and the ground was completely soaked through. There was mud everywhere, and moving around on the site was difficult due to its poor ground conditions. We unloaded the panels one by one and connected them to the foundation piers via a screw jack. We

FROM LEFT: Rice students loading prefabricated panels onto truck. Rice students installing floor panels. Second floor framing completed. View of house from Project Row Houses.

used this detail to allow for the necessary adjustment required to level the floor panels over the ensuing weeks, when Houston's forever moving soils caused some settling to occur. With a few turns of a wrench, and with little difficulty, we were able to adjust each floor panel height. To fasten the floor panels to the middle foundation piers, some of us braver souls had to slither under what would eventually be the crawl space under the house. By the time we got out from underneath the panels, our backs were covered in mud, and it was definitely time for a shower. Yet we were able to set all the floor panels that first day and it was exciting to see the beginnings of what would be the first floor of the new house.

A few crews of students worked several days a week to get the house framed up. This went relatively quickly, since it was just a matter of assembling the already fabricated wood panels. Some specialized framing was done on-site, as well as roofing and waterproofing, but for the most part the skeleton of the house was built prior to arriving on-site, which expedited the schedule for the first few months. At the rate we were going, it appeared as though the house would be completed before we knew it, and someone would be able to make it a home. Little did we know just how long the remainder of the construction effort would take. We quickly learned that not all things go according to plan or fit as they were originally intended. Sometimes we did not have the proper tools for certain tasks, which increased the time it took to do those tasks. Details had to be changed on-site due to field conditions.

Over the course of the construction process, we got to know our neighbors. The mothers and children living in nearby residences at Project Row Houses met us with numerous questions: "What are you building?" and "What's it going to look like?" We looked forward to seeing them from week to week. When we stopped in at the corner market for a drink or a snack, we were greeted with, "How's the house coming?" and "It's looking great out there." If we did not stop by the market in awhile, we were asked, "Where've you been? Haven't seen you in awhile." We were invited to the many functions held in courtyards at Project

Interior showing living room/stair, and door to the back porch with loft above.

Row Houses, from barbecues to blues concerts. It felt as though we all were becoming a part of this community.

Once the semester ended, the work crews got a lot smaller. The Rice Building Workshop would begin a new project for its next semester, so completion of the house would be done on a volunteer basis. This meant working only on weekends—usually Saturdays, with an occasional Sunday thrown in from time to time. In the beginning volunteers were plentiful, but as time passed, it came down to a core group of individuals who stuck with it to the end. No one had anticipated just how long a project of this scale would take for "unskilled" laborers. It was a large commitment and could be draining at times, as it seemed we never got anywhere, but it was also an incredible learning experience. Observing our progress over time was priceless, and I think everyone who worked on this project walked away feeling a sense of pride about belonging to something really special.

A huge collaborative effort made the house possible and worthwhile. Project Row Houses was a constant source of encouragement and thanks for the work we were doing. They helped raise funds, provided us with a space for our tools and supplies, and offered help whenever time allowed. A retired structural engineer shared his professional expertise and asked nothing in return. Various companies donated materials at no cost. Local unions trained apprentices on the job and completed all plumbing and electrical requirements for the house with no charge, and area professionals donated their skills and time to help with the final finishing touches. Two former students returned to share some of their metal working skills by creating a beautiful handrail at the stair and a balcony off the second floor. It was amazing to see how willing everyone was to make donations of all kinds and come together to achieve a common goal.

A HOUSE AT LAST

As construction neared completion, we all wondered who would be housed here and to what part of Project Row Houses this house would belong. It was a pleasant surprise to find out that the house would become part of the single mothers' residences, and the lucky inhabitant-to-be was someone we had all come to know over the course of the project. She was a volunteer at Project Row Houses who once lived in the community and always dreamed of someday returning. She supplied us with words of encouragement and even helped out with some painting. She and I used to banter back and forth about how we would fight each other to see who got to live in the house, so I was really excited when I found out she would be its resident. I knew the house meant as much, if not more, to her as it did to me, and I was happy to know it would be appreciated and given to someone truly deserving. She and her family loved their new home and had nothing but wonderful things to say about it. To this day, she remarks, "If I have my say, I will never move from this house." She mentioned that she may have filled in some of the double-height squares for more storage space or another bedroom, but later said she liked it the way it is, generous space and all. She could not thank us enough for providing something that for so long had only been a dream to her family. That alone made all the hard work worth it in the end.

We shared our project with the community through several open-house tours and received comments from the public at large on the work we had done there. It was so rewarding to hear all the positive feedback on the design of the house. Such an undertaking by college students and young professionals impressed the community, and we were all thankful that the house was well received.

We had achieved our original intention for the design: to create a smaller home with the quality and livability of a much larger one. Corner windows opened up views to the outside, toward Project Row Houses and downtown Houston, and created a visual and physical connection between the two. High ceilings made rooms appear much larger than they actually were and afforded a lot more natural light. The squares were designed as efficiently as possible and created an open flow between spaces.

When I look back on this project, I have nothing but positive memories, with the exception of the seemingly never-ending construction schedule. I revisit my photos documenting the project from start to finish every now and then, and remember how I once participated in a collaborative effort to further an already impressive vision and achieve a common goal. The camaraderie we all shared and the respect we all had for each other while devoting our weekends to work on the project are irreplaceable. In the years since, I have not yet once been inspired by the sense of place and community that lived on there, and I long someday to find it again. I hope that sharing these projects and experiences with others might encourage them to attempt similar projects throughout the world and provide an outlet for designers, young and old, to share their design expertise with society and help shape its future.

ARCHEWORKS
MONICA CHADHA

Archeworks, an independent educational program, seeks out special needs that fall under the radar, then develops prototypes to serve them. This project, a kitchen for wheelchair users, shows what creativity can do for a very familiar problem.

MONICA CHADHA was the facilitator for the team at Archeworks. She has a background in architecture and participatory design.

Increasingly, young designers desire to balance the practical experience that collaboration brings with the paper architecture of traditional schools. A highly successful model of this pedagogy exists at an alternative design school in Chicago called Archeworks, which develops design solutions to diverse social needs through an interdisciplinary approach and user experimentation.

Stanley Tigerman and Eva Maddox founded Archeworks in 1993 to provide design solutions to sectors of society whose needs are rarely served, such as the physically disabled, the homeless, young offenders, and the elderly. The school addresses social needs by developing and implementing design solutions through a multidisciplinary process. Students come to the nine-month program from a variety of educational and practical backgrounds such as architecture, business, law, industrial design, and nursing. Each team is made up of students with different proficiencies, and thus each project is approached from multiple perspectives. I and the other facilitator (instructor) at the school encourage students to build upon one another's expertise in an effort to evolve a design solution.

Teams are partnered with clients in a community. Funding is allotted to each team, which allows students to work with the community organizations. Projects are completed when they are installed or distributed to the user. Archeworks students have designed and installed low-cost furniture for the formerly homeless at a single-residence-occupancy building; disseminated a journal, *Hinge*, on intergenerational issues; and participated in community revitalization in Chicago's West Humboldt Park neighborhood through the design and building of a community garden, gateway, and banners. A number of projects have gone beyond serving their original user and have been widely distributed, such as a head pointer for people with cerebral palsy (sold in the Sammons Preston catalog) and a welcome kit for new social workers (to be distributed throughout the Chicago area).

One recently completed project was a kitchen design that serves the need of the physically challenged. Archeworks partnered with Access Living, an advocacy group for the physically disabled, for this task. In their initial meeting with the students, the client asked the students to come up with an ideal accessible home design. Given the difficulty of this proposal, the students instigated a series of meetings and discussions to define a more manageable task. They learned that the advocacy group was seeking innovative and inexpensive design solutions to show that it is possible to go beyond the Americans with Disabilities Act (ADA) and create accessible spaces that are integrated with their surroundings.

THE PROCESS

Students began the term with in-depth research. Several members of the team explored existing accessible products and housing for the disabled. They quickly established that many items in production were created only as a function of need and were neither aesthetically appealing nor marketed to the general public. A notable exception is the widely distributed OXO line of kitchen products, which were initially designed for people with physical impairments.

Other students began to explore existing guidelines and requirements for accessible housing. While the students were aiming to meet Access Living's desires, they also realized the difficulty of fulfilling their request to design a single solution for accessibility. As the team began to define criteria for universal design, they realized how difficult it was to determine even that. To come up with one design solution to meet the needs of all would be impossible, and so the students adopted the concept of "mass customization"—exploring a universal solution that could be modified by an individual to meet that person's specific needs and desires.

By the end of the research phase, the students had not yet defined a product. At this point, I challenged them to use a participatory design process to achieve a solution. Participatory design involves engaging the end user in the design process. Working closely with the end users, the students sought to determine the precise design need and what types of solutions would work.

The students initiated a series of focus groups to further define the project. The first focus group defined where there was a pressing need for improved accessibility. Participants were asked which household tasks were most difficult and worked on exercises that compared their current housing situation to the "ideal home." From their answers, the students saw that there was a need for "beautiful" design rather than jerry-rigged solutions. The participants also felt that the kitchen was an area of the house where they encountered the most usage problems. The participants also questioned whether solutions designed for someone with a physical impairment had to look different. They desired solutions that did not carry the stigmatization of being designed for the disabled.

Site visits showing, for example that upper cabinets were difficult to reach from a wheelchair confirmed the need for a more accessible kitchen design. Students were shown existing design solutions that were not effective such as a hole in a countertop to stabilize a mixing bowl, which only worked if its user had a very specific bowl). The students began to study how disabled people moved and realized that feet, elbows, and canes, and not just hands, could perform certain motions. They prepared a series of hinged, sliding, and rotating prototypes for a new focus group, who explored the models and helped create material palettes. Their exploration of materials and colors further emphasized the need for a solution that could be customized by the individual.

By winter term, the students were working on models and sketches for a customizable kitchen. It took until the beginning of spring term for the students to collectively reach their initial design. In the words of one team member, Jitendre Barlinge, "In the traditional model of the kitchen, there has always been intense focus by architects and designers to minimize the movement in the work triangle. Even that level of movement can be difficult for someone with limited mobility. The first step was to rethink the activity of working in the kitchen. It became necessary to collapse the kitchen work triangle in order to reduce the movement to zero."

The students first developed a six-foot-diameter cylindrical kitchen unit. Its storage requirements and elements were based on existing kitchens, time and motion studies, and by testing out recipes. While this model maximized available storage, the full-scale mockup of the design came under serious criticism from a focus group. None of the participants were convinced of its workability. Its size was unwieldy, and its benefit over a typical kitchen was not clear. At this point in its design, the unit did not clearly demonstrate the ability to meet the user's need, nor did it seem likely to become a mass-produced product. The focus group made a number of suggestions that were incorporated into the design, including reducing the unit's overall size and creating distinct storage and cooking modules. Thus, "Kurumono" was born. The unit finally succeeded in showing that the kitchen could be redefined. It was no longer necessary for someone to move about the kitchen; the kitchen could rotate, spin, or lower itself toward the user.

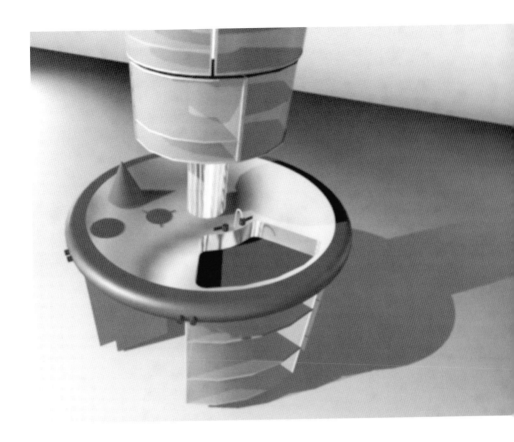

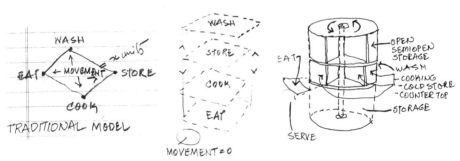

TOP: *Kurumono* kitchen unit allows elements to rotate and accommodates a wheelchair. ABOVE LEFT: Diagram of traditional kitchen showing travel distance between each function. ABOVE CENTER: Proposed schematic concept by a student after research phase shows increased proximity between kitchen functions. ABOVE RIGHT: Student design sketch of final project showing functions and their locations.

PRODUCT DESCRIPTION

Kurumono is a Japanese word meaning "everything comes to you." The students designed a modular cylindrical unit made up of three sections: upper cabinets, worktop, and lower modules containing sink, dishwasher, and refrigerator. These sections rotate around a centrally located pole that houses all plumbing, electrical supply, and ventilation facilities.

A hydraulic system allows each section to rotate and slide as required by the user to be positioned at a comfortable and accessible distance. The upper cabinets can be lowered to the comfort zone, and additional flip-out worktops ensure that all storage is accessible and counter space is maximized. The students had learned from the focus groups that different uses deal with technology differently. They designed Kurumono to embody a manual option, allowing each person to choose how to use the unit. The unit would be embedded with a microprocessor and memory to enable the machine to remember and replicate the users' patterns. This "smart" technology could also be used to track which grocery items are depleted, alerting the user when it is time for a trip to the supermarket and printing out a shopping list.

The students envisioned a kitchen environment that would work efficiently. Similar to a doctor who relies on the medical team to perform surgery, the user could rely on the kitchen itself to make the implements available and place them within reach. Kurumono's modularity allows for easy arrangement of the sections as well as continued customization over time. The user can add or eliminate units and change color palettes or surface textures. The ability to customize materials can benefit the visually impaired by providing highly contrasting surfaces and textured edges to denote change.

The students envisioned a new way of thinking about access in the kitchen and reduced the traditional work triangle to zero. This represents a quantum leap in design not only for people who are elderly or have mobility impairments, arthritis, or other difficulties, but also for the able-bodied.

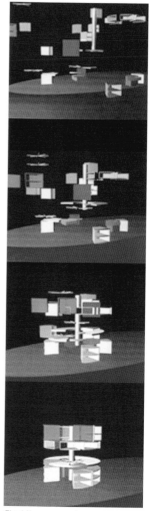

Final *Kurumono* scheme.

PRODUCT EVOLUTION

The spring term was spent refining the design and streamlining the functions that would be included in the kitchen. Through three-dimensional modeling and scale prototyping, Kurumono continued to evolve. At the final review, there was a positive response to the product. A number of attendees expressed a desire for Kurumono to replace their conventional kitchens. It was only through a continuous exchange between the users and involved professionals that the students were able to push the design to this level. The team then established a Website to disseminate their findings and make the information widely available. While this site serves as an information tool to Access Living, Archeworks is pursuing further funding to build a fully functioning prototype of the design. The long-term goal is to put Kurumono into mass production.

SMALL TOWN CENTER
SHANNON CRISS

Public space making—even with a great economy of means such as this small park project—can go a long way in reinforcing communities, as well as forming relationships between designers and community members.

SHANNON CRISS is associate professor at the University of Kansas School of Architecture and Urban Design. Previously, she was an associate professor and the director of the Small Town Center at Mississippi State University's School of Architecture.

Okolona, Mississippi, is a town of three thousand located in northeast Mississippi. Once a prosperous railroad town and trading center, it in recent years has become a bedroom community for people working in nearby Tupelo. The public image of the town has declined over the past few years, as buildings suffer neglect through disinvestment, and as the town's limited resources are spent on "essentials" like schools and police, not on maintaining the public realm. Like other small Mississippi towns, Okolona was once a (legally) racially segregated town, with whites living on one side of town and African-Americans on the other. This community continually works to find opportunities to bridge the gap that still exists between the races, and recognizes the need to revitalize its economic base and invest in its public space.

A PARK FOR OKOLONA

In 1997, a small group of concerned citizens—both black and white—met to discuss the idea of building a small park in downtown Okolona, in a location that neither race would "own." They envisioned the park as a common ground that would provide the community with a collaborative project on which to focus its energies in a highly public manner during planning and construction. It could be a place for public events, such as church performances, school events, a farmers market, and election rallies. They also desired a space with shade for the occasional passerby or a lunch break.

This 140-by-50-foot site at Main and a major cross street linked diverse neighborhoods and served as a neutral site for the community. My students in the design-build program at Mississippi State University joined with local community members to provide the ground for a shared, tangible result. The project embraced the thoughts and suggestions of many people. The greater the number of people involved, with their viewpoints helping to shape the project, the greater the possibility that the physical place would hold significance and foster future use for those in the community. By establishing principles internal to the place and the people, a better fit is possible.

The students began by immersing themselves in the neighborhoods, using sketches and photography to record and become familiar with this place. This forced the students to transform their own feelings of being outsiders into something that could assist the design of the park. They were not aware of the subtle racial boundaries in the community and were motivated to walk around and take photos of those things that seemed curious to them. They found creative ways in which people transformed commonplace objects into yard art, fences, and signs, which ultimately helped them discover new potential for commonplace materials such as re-bar, parking bumpers, and abandoned farming tools. The students' initial research into the community was not always easy or pleasant. Several were questioned as to why they were there, why they were taking photos. During discussions back at school, many students revealed that they were not certain we should be there, that many felt uncomfortable with our "intrusion" into the town. Class morale was beginning to suffer.

At that point Patsy Gregory, the director of the Okolona Area Chamber of Commerce and the primary figure in getting this park off the ground, organized a diverse group of citizens— young and old, black and white, newcomers and long-term residents—to meet with us to share their feelings about Okolona. We gathered one evening in the town hall, and the residents took turns telling their stories. Some recounted their several-generation family histories in the town; others why they so desperately wanted to get Okolona out of its "funk"; others the bright future they imagined for the town. At times it got emotional, and the evening ended with a very noticeable change in the students' attitudes. It was easy to see that some people in Okolona did appreciate our presence, were optimistic about our efforts, and were going to be supportive during the construction. It was a critical moment.

Immersing ourselves into the community had another effect—we gained an appreciation for local creative design that inspired our own work. Many Okolonians make do with limited resources and must rely upon modest means to express themselves in their surroundings. They collect and stockpile things with the sense that they may someday come in handy. Things are contingent, as there is not a definite plan; everything has potential.

FROM RESEARCH TO DESIGN

Following this, the students started designing schemes for their vision of the park. Decision making during the design process was governed by the idea of consensus building. Collaborative efforts did not come easy, as the typical architectural education emphasizes original thought and individual creative acts. Getting all thirty-two students to share and develop ideas was only possible through a series of discussions. Many of these discussions were

A student assists community children with a paving project.

tested in community gatherings, challenged by real, practical concerns. Playing out ideas within the presence of those that lived in Okolona helped the students focus and avoid making fantastic, unachievable suggestions. The students built a highly crafted, large model of the park proposal and displayed it in a downtown storefront. Making the ideas public helped the general community understand what we were about to undertake and forced the students to be clear with their intentions.

All students in the class proposed individual schemes for the park at the beginning of the design phase. From these, we identified large principles that were embedded in numerous schemes: shading, sitting, performance, edge-making, vegetation, etc. When we reached consensus on a set of principles, the class divided itself up into teams to develop specific solutions to address these principles. In this way the students designed the specific elements for the park: a wisteria arbor, a stage, benches, a retaining wall, and paving to address a rift between two existing concrete slabs.

We were inspired by the way the community used found objects and materials in new, improvised ways, and designed the arbor out of half-inch reinforcing bar that wrapped the steel members and were assembled to make columns and vaults. The arbor is seventy-by-ten feet, strengthened by interlocking pieces and anchored to footings. We installed up-lighting on the columns and in the ground for evening use. The wisteria combats the extreme summer heat and provides shade. In a town such as Okolona where the tax base is relatively low, maintaining a park is not the highest priority. In designing the park we had to consider how the materials and assemblies would age.

Working with common materials and a low-skilled labor force is the way many of our Mississippi buildings get built. And in our case, our own low skills put us to the test. We built a one-hundred-foot retaining wall to contain the edge of the slab and conform to the changing slope of the site out of stacked concrete parking bumpers and anchored by steel angles. Instead of relying on skilled brick- or stonemasons, we used this common, affordable material (nineteen dollars per bumper) that became more elegant through repetition and its subtle shadows.

TOP: Overview of park in Okolona, Mississippi, including a wisteria arbor, a stage, benches, a retaining wall, and paving. ABOVE: The retaining wall is made of concrete parking bumpers and angled steel.

TOP: A student welds steel in place at the wisteria arbor. ABOVE: Wisteria is beginning to grow on the arbor.

Understanding the needs and desires of various citizens and how to incorporate those ideas came at different moments in the design process. As we began to transform the site with demolition and to pour footings, people in general would stop and question what we were doing. A local carpenter took an interest in our work, participated in its construction, and, in effect, taught the students some skills of his trade. One woman who lived down the alleyway adjacent to the park was highly skeptical at first of our work. She did not think it was possible to develop what we planned to build. However, as she became familiar with some of the students and spent time watching what they were doing day by day, she saw how committed they were to the project. As a result, she organized a weekly meal in her home, involving many neighbors in the cooking. Through

John Bondurant, Barry Lann, and Kyle Kish work on the arbor.

these social gatherings, the word spread and more people took interest and stopped at the site. Practically every day that we were on site, someone would stop and drop off a cooler of Cokes or a platter of cookies. With such connection to the community, the students were offered opinions, suggestions, and skills that strengthened the park proposal. Following group approval of the basic elements, the teams began building mockups for a town meeting at midterm to receive community feedback and approval. We learned to represent our ideas there in ways that were direct and easy to understand; clear communication helped us establish relationships and secure the involvement of local people. We realized their involvement was critical to the future life and the usefulness of the park.

As the project progressed, students took on different leadership roles and responsibilities: one developed project management methods, while another negotiated with suppliers. Project needs directed the students' energy and focus. Students found their specific role in the project according to their interest and aptitude.

DESIGN PRINCIPLES

The method of critiquing the students' designs was based on internal principles of the place, such as use, durability, and time, rather than strictly on form and appearance. Designing *and* building, back and forth, provide the potential for a more sincere product and innovation. This process provided space for experimentation and improvisation, and in these, architecture may rediscover craft and the potential of materials. It brings a degree of outside reality that allows our work to be more relevant to broader, more public concerns.[1]

The very act of making something in this way places a higher regard on the act itself. Learning to improvise and respond to the conditions and material at hand provides an important lesson. By slowing down and seeing the potential of a place and its people, we remake ourselves to fit the circumstances at hand; we approach our work in a different manner, and this can be enormously instructive.[2]

[1] Some of the thoughts included in this paper, are informed by "Working Space: Notes on Design Studio Work in the Public Realm," a paper that David Perkes, associate professor at Mississippi State University, and I developed and delivered at the National Association of Collegiate Schools of Architecture in Cleveland, Ohio, in the spring of 1998.

[2] The project is not developed by our internal motivations, but instead by collaborating with others—designers and community participants—we are forced to find shared, basic motivations for design. In this way we search for those characteristics and connections that are outside our past experiences and find form and purpose that are foreign to us. In effect, we remake ourselves. It is difficult to enact this attitude and way of working in the architectural academic setting.

3 Michael Benedikt, "Less for Less Yet: On Architecture's Value(s) in the Marketplace," *Designer/Builder* (October 1999): 21–26.

4 The term "loose fit" helped to communicate the need for flexibility in designing that would allow for more options and a broader concern for form. By defining a working space in which others could participate, the project was truly shaped by multiple and conflicting viewpoints. A loose fit optimized the built forms by generosity, inclusiveness, flexibility, and the search for enduring and intangible qualities. "Loose fit" is a term that Professor Chris Risher of Mississippi State University often uses, although he would undoubtedly have a more eloquent definition of it.

Our authority over our work is challenged. Working with others exposes our personal thoughts and challenges us to make structures that can be inhabited by others. As Michael Benedict has written, "The very act of making, working to both gain an appreciation of the technical and poetic qualities of the things made, helps us to make a powerful case that architecture matters."[3] The work's authority is no longer that of the individual, but relies on broader concerns that are internal to the problem, such as the flexibility of form to allow for a diversity of uses, the durability of materials and assembly to endure the rain, heat, and wind, the impromptu use of the stage and potential other uses, the budget of $24,000 for materials for the 6,500-square-foot site, and the ability to share an idea among thirty-two students and a community. So often, the practice of architecture instead errs in its single-minded approach.

A new confidence emerges from the context of uncertainties as designers rely upon their own beliefs and values, reconfirming them in the act of building. I believe that such is the critical value of working in public ways. This park was conceived as being able to both shape and hold imaginative qualities. In this project we realized that a looser fit between the original intent and the final product was truer and more sincere to the needs of the site and the community.[4]

Through this kind of work, we have come to understand how critical it is to involve the community in the life of our projects; it is not possible for a design to be cared for and maintained without a community taking possession of it. This looser fit between architect, builder, and user suspends the design process to involve others in it early on, which provides the grounding for many to be involved and able to pursue long-term community making. The practice of designing and building allow others to be involved in tangible ways and establishes the place for long-term community making. Through the

Design studio class at opening day.

process of making this park, the community found an opportunity to reestablish their relationships to one another, to see the ugliness and invalidity of racist viewpoints and the opportunity to invent a new shared, public life. Involving many in the making of the park provided a powerful case that architecture does indeed matter.

KU STUDIO 804
JESSICA BRISTOW

At the University of Kansas, the graduating Master of Architecture students undertake to completely design and build a home in the final four and a half months of the program. The goal of Studio 804 is to apply sustainable and dynamic materials in both traditional and non-traditional methods in a project that combines academic training with the practicalities of the craft of building.

JESSICA BRISTOW is a freelance writer and architectural designer in Lawrence, Kansas. Having completed her Master of Architecture, she is currently finishing a second master's degree in art history. She intends to continue in an art history Ph.D. program.

DAY 1

Sixteen architecture graduate students return early from a winter break to attack the final design studio of the Master of Architecture program at the University of Kansas. Energized by the goal to design and build an innovative, economical, ADA-accessible environment, we come together to pool our resources into a single design. We have shortened our break with the hope of having a design to present to our client at their board meeting in one week.

This is possible because we began our task in the previous semester. Our work in the fall included meeting with the Tenants to Homeowners Association (TTH) of Lawrence, Kansas, to determine the overall program of the project and the dispersal of funding. To help raise funds our design-build program, Studio 804, is organized as a nonprofit 501(c)(3) organization. TTH receives a community development block grant that also helps fund our project, and the studio obtains all other funding through donated or discounted materials and free labor. TTH works to sell homes at an extremely reduced cost to qualified low-income families with disabilities.

Before breaking ground, Studio 804 met daily at the University of Kansas to discuss design and business.

Until the end of the process, our actual client is a nameless, faceless set of circumstances. We design for the most intensely need-based scenario: universal accessibility. It is possible that our future owner will be severely disabled. For this reason, we decide to make the home as low maintenance as possible. The limited income of our client also informs our decision to design energy efficiency into our choice of materials.

DAY 3

During our first days back we discuss individual models. We produce constructs of our ideas at an amazing pace and present new ideas every day. We argue and debate as we try to sell our own solutions to the group. After reviewing many dozens of models, we narrow the program into two basic forms: a wedge and a ramp. Complete design agreement may seem like an impossibility; stubborn minds and vulnerable egos can cause strife in the most cohesive of groups. But because of the pace of the design process, we must simply shove that aside. We must maintain a democratic approach. We experiment quickly to sort the creative solutions from the problems. Our small site has made it impossible to place the entire 1,500 square feet with attached garage on a single story and maintain the necessary setbacks. We experiment with detaching the garage from the main structure and dividing the home into two separate volumes, then decide it is a necessity to move onto a design with a second floor.

DAY 6

We begin our daily four-hour meetings with business updates. While continuing with the design, we are also continuing our drive to acquire discounted and donated materials, to post a Website to increase visibility, to determine the plat of the site with the city, to organize information, and to research ADA compliance and new materials. All the while, we continually search for funding. We have set before ourselves the most monumental job of multitasking. It is obvious that this home will dominate our lives for the duration of its conception.

We make refinements to our two plans until it has come time to make our decision. Our wedge shape has a pleasing proportion and a certain ease of construction in its formal simplicity. Our ramp design accentuates the accessibility inherent in the proposal but also creates problems in engineering and expense. The question "How will we build that?" lies heavily on our minds. We work overnight on these issues and return the next morning to take a vote. With an inaudible sigh of relief, we end the debate with the comfortable buildability of the wedge. With two days before our meeting with TTH, we scurry to update the drawings and construct a model. If they accept our design, we can move forward and develop the building process.

DAY 8

A nervous sense of trepidation ripples through the group as we await the start of our project meeting with Tenants to Homeowners. Past projects of Studio 804 have met with some resistance from city officials and neighborhood groups; our focus on design and materials has brought conservative criticism on everything from the color of the exterior material to the simplicity of the overall form. Because of this, we choose to focus our presentation not on the specific choice of materials, but on our concern for ease of maintenance and reusing or recycling materials. We consciously agree not to solicit input regarding design decisions.

Our concern is unwarranted. TTH has been extremely supportive of our creativity throughout the early stages of the process, and during the meeting their attitude remains consistent. They focus the discussion on the necessity for the ADA compliance of the entire house to facilitate their acquisition of funding. The local residents want to improve their neighborhood by reducing the number of undesirable rental houses, and so for them the benefits of an owner-occupied home far outweigh any concern over its appearance. We revel in the fact that our new client allows us to express our creativity. With this renewed sense of support and motivation, we return to the studio to continue the design.

DAY 10

After we finalize the main form, we divide our group in order to address the varied materials of the project. As individuals or groups, we research recycled materials, the details of concrete work, foundation and roof construction, wall framing, HVAC, and material sources. The results of our findings help in the design of the structural details. At this point we refine the proportions and finalize the plan.

Our wedge form now includes a loftlike second floor dedicated to a master bedroom, which could be used by a caregiver for someone with a severe disability. The loft necessitates a stairway that must be equipped with a chairlift. The two bathrooms of the program are stacked and designed with a steel structure to form an interior core that breaks the open space of the main form and provides a focal point in the design. A bridge connects the second-floor bathroom to the bedroom. We have begun to think conceptually of the home as a lantern of life. The open outer wood-framed section reveals the public side of the home while the solid enclosed areas contain the private. Issues of hidden versus revealed confront us in every decision.

DAY 17

In past years Studio 804 has published a booklet for each of its projects. This publication not only documents the design and process, but also serves as a potent inspiration for us and an

For ease of construction, the walls are framed on the floor decks before being fitted into place.

invaluable tool in our search for funding. The project would never come to be without our donated labor and the savings in material and services that we are able to acquire from the local community and construction industries. We credit every donor in the booklet and provide each with a copy. In this way we hope to build a relationship with those who support us in order for our studio to continue functioning.

We must all assist in searching for materials and donations. We distribute the booklet on the previous project, and then immediately begin compiling our own and constructing a new Website. Our choice and innovative use of material and the quality of our design and construction allows us to submit our design for competitions, which are other sources of valuable exposure for the project and our contributors. We form a publication group and the rest of us move outside into the cold winter.

DAY 24

Moving outside has some motivational power. The weather holds, sunny but brisk, as we stake out the site, excavate it, and build the concrete forms for the foundation. We set a date and order the concrete. We meet at seven A.M. in the icy drizzle of February to pour concrete. We wade in a slop of mud and shiver as our clothes are soaked and the chill reaches our bones. The arduous aspects of building have already begun to materialize. With this dreary beginning, the process seems to loom before us. Wary of the weather, we return four days later to remove the snow-covered strawbales and carefully strip the concrete forms so that we can reuse the plywood sheathing. The lumber arrives and we set out to frame the wedge.

We sheath the floor in twenty-degree weather, keeping the brisk wind to our backs. We frame the walls on the floor deck and sweep snow from them in the morning. Those of us on the site begin to envy our publications group. We use two-by-six studs to increase the insulation and energy efficiency of the structure. We sheath and apply a water barrier to the individual walls before they are set in place. With disbelief and anticipation, the walls go up and the wedge begins to take form, even though we have not yet firmly decided on the exterior skin. The loft floor goes in. We lift the sixteen-foot wall with its giant window header carefully in place. Hesitantly, we climb to the peak and frame the roof. We pour the garage floor, driveway, and sidewalk. As we work, our only subcontractors—electrical, HVAC, and plumbing—work among us. Our individual responsibilities make us all testy and disagreeable.

The issue of money is ever present in our process, as our budget has been inadequate since the outset. While we want to maximize the space for living, we must constantly look to the tectonic details and the creative use of materials to bring richness to such a small space. We learn that we can obtain a redwood cooling tower in Coffeyville as a donation if we remove it ourselves. We use parts of it as a sunscreen on the south side of the house to minimize cooling costs and other parts on the north-facing front facade to create continuity. It provides a necessary change in scale that reduces the overall appearance of mass of the structure. We now have to design a structure to support it.

Spring break is here, but we continue on our task. We design details directly as we build. "Mock-up" becomes the word of the hour. The design of the interior steel core is finalized following the initial full-scale building attempt. We find a source for transparent polycarbonate that will skin the interior structure, and investigate a translucent paint to coat the surface of the Lexan for privacy. TTH informs us that four families with disabilities have applied and are qualified for our home.

We are acquiring materials at a feverish pace. We need everything today. The sheets for our low-maintenance Cor-Ten steel skin are being cut and are on their way. We have found a gymnasium floor that is ours if we, once again, remove it. We cut it into twenty-foot strips and haul it away still attached to its plywood underlayment. This increases our floor height, and we so must raise all the headers. In the woodshop, we build all the cabinetry for the home.

All walls, including this two-story structural steel framed bathroom core wall, are raised as a group.

April arrives with the sun, and our May 20 graduation deadline looms before us. We seal the exterior water barrier and apply flashing. In stocking feet, we apply the rubber roof. We build the steel frames for the decks and paint them, then cut redwood from the cooling tower and create panels for the deck floors. We build steel brackets for the sunscreen and attach them perched on scaffolding. We drill and fit the Cor-Ten, and the smooth form shines in the sun. We fit the redwood screen, lay the flooring, fit the windows, and hang the

LEFT: Once the structure is completely enclosed, Studio 804 can work late into the evening on the interior finishes. RIGHT: A view of the completed bathroom core, showing the stairs and cabinets that create a sense of privacy within the loft.

doors. Painstakingly, we fill and sand the screw holes in the floor so that we do not have to refinish it. Building and finishing has become a scurry of activity.

TTH chooses a single mother and her children to purchase the home. Because of her multiple disabilities, she receives a government grant to pay the low cost that TTH has given her. She will be able to live here for free.

DAY 105

The tension rises. Someone has not been here all day. Someone does not work very hard. How did this get messed up? We hate these fixtures. Where are the bathtubs? Where is the Lexan? It seems as if the number of tasks increases every minute. The crunch of materials and time requires long hours and a fast pace. We tick off jobs one by one. We take care now to finish with an extreme attention to detail. We avoid interior molding by fitting the gypsum board with great precision. The bathroom skin glows green from within. The cabinets hang and float within our perfect white interior form. The surfaces are cleaned. Our new owner and her children visit late one day. We give her a tour and watch her face light up as her children play on the deck. We know now that she will love it as much as we do. Nothing will ever compare to this.

A view of the finished southwest corner; the Cor-Ten has only begun to show its final patina.

DAY 124

In our final morning meeting, we stand back and notice that the grass has filled in and the Cor-Ten has rusted as intended and glows like a flame before us. We all sigh from relief and pride. We have survived mutiny and attack. We all find it amazing that we have been able to create this innovative design without having any one person in charge or any one person leading the design. It has been, in totality, a group effort. Somewhere deep inside we think, "It is finished," sadly.

Our accomplishments in this project provide us with courage to face any challenge. Studio 804 allows and forces us to deal with varied personalities and the tensions of scheduling time. By building what we design, we learn the value of craftsmanship and the beauty of tectonics. We see more clearly the creativity that can be found in the use of new materials or the new use of existing materials. We see the beauty in an architecture that has less impact on the environment. We understand that a low-income project is not necessarily a detriment to design, and accommodating accessibility issues not a hindrance but a necessity to the comfort of any space. The main impact of this studio is that, like any first-time experience, its effect will stay with us and surface in our memories again and again.

OUTREACH STUDIO
MARCUS HURLEY

In the summer of 1999, Samuel Mockbee and Bryan Bell founded the Outreach Studio to expand the benefits of the Rural Studio to non–Auburn University students studying a variety of disciplines. In this essay, Marcus Hurley reflects on his experience and his motivation for attending the program.

MARCUS HURLEY is an architect in Washington, D.C. He holds a master's degree from the University of Virginia and participated in the first Outreach Studio during the summer of 2000.

Auburn University's 2000 Outreach Studio brought together seven fellows with the intent of pursuing independent research projects related to their respective disciplines—which included architecture, education, public health, sociology, and waste water management—as well as collaborating on a design-build project. We each had our own motivations for volunteering our efforts, but over the course of our ten weeks together, I uncovered unexpected ideas about my work in Alabama's Black Belt.

I set off for the town of Mason's Bend that summer with the words of my graduation speech weighing heavily on my mind. The speaker, Andy Rooney, said the best reply to the question, "So what are you going to do now?" was "I'm going to do the things that need to get done in the world." His generation defended the world from the tyranny of Nazi Germany and the Soviet Union. Rooney told the latest batch of college graduates that what needed to get done today was no less important—it just was not nearly as obvious. My experience in Alabama showed me that at least one of the important tasks that face my generation is to use available resources to help bring the poorest member of our society at least onto the playing field. I decided that my part would begin among those nearest to the bottom of the ladder, in Hale County, Alabama.

A GROUP PROJECT

It was not long after I arrived that I found myself faced with the difficulties of carrying out my independent research project: to manage a design-build studio with an overwhelming

Outreach students building rammed-earth shelter.

cache of ideas and needs, a more-than-adequate budget, and eager labor, but only a short amount of time. My colleagues and I surveyed the Mason's Bend residents for their ideas as to what most needed to be done, but at the time I think we undervalued their empirical knowledge of the community in favor of our own theories. One of the greatest difficulties we met was combining input from the various parties—fellows, residents, professionals, etc.—who influenced the design process with my own ideas about the project. I had to remind myself that I am only one part of a design team whose expertise encompasses a greater scope than my own individual experience.

We were lucky that enough of the residents presented the same concerns that, eventually, we began to really listen. One recurring idea was a recreation space for the community's youngest members. At the time, the focus of the children's activities was a makeshift basketball court on the main road leading into Mason's Bend. We discovered that the Department of Transportation had designated the road for improvement that fall, rendering the site unsafe. A relocated permanent court would not only build upon a popular recreational activity, but would also allow a safer alternative for the local children than playing in the new street. We chose the site and materials for the new court to complement both the adjacent community chapel designed and built by thesis students in Auburn's Rural Studio program, as well as the surrounding community. Our choice to use vernacular rather than exotic materials saved us a lot of time, effort, and money during the building process. The materials—such as corrugated galvanized metal used frequently in the area, stock-structural steel used in the catfish farming industry, and a common "road mix" soil of red clay and aggregate—were readily available in large supply to our site, which we discovered was incredibly remote. Using local materials also made expertise and advice available in large supply to our group of construction novices.

Outreach students building school bus shelter and basketball half court in Mason's Bend, Alabama.

Not all aspects of the program went so smoothly. I discovered that I had to approach each task with more than enough enthusiasm to weather setbacks and disappointments, and that the effectiveness of a group effort relies most heavily on the amount of coordination. However, I also found the need to exercise a balance between sticking to the coordinated plan and adapting to changing conditions. At one point, we were faced with a problem that was best solved by just such a balance. Scheduling dictated that the steel roof structure for our project had to be erected on a certain date. We worked hard to prepare the project to receive the roof by that date, but on the appointed day, the steel supplier delivered insufficient lengths of the required steel members. Given the fact that the professional welders we required to safely erect the roof structure were only available that day, it seemed as if a major setback was upon us. But rather than focus solely on the problem, we bypassed the situation by choosing a new solution. (I am still surprised at how much of the summer and my subsequent career experience is based on choosing from the available options.) On a welder's advice, we decided to splice the shorter members into a single beam long enough to complete the job. I was skeptical of the splice's effectiveness, but I trusted the steel professional's empirical knowledge. By day's end, the roof structure was successfully topped out, and I had a first-hand experience of steel splicing (bolstered in no small part by the welder walking out to the end of the spliced beam we erected dangerously high above the ground).

THE OBJECTIVE OF OUR WORK

Over the course of the summer, I thought a great deal about what I was trying to accomplish by the end of my time in Mason's Bend. Of course, one of my primary goals was to see the design-build idea through to some kind of useful product. However, I wanted the project to continue to grow and develop after we left the Outreach Studio. My thoughts on this subject were constantly changing throughout much of my experience.

Seeing the living conditions that were all too common in Mason's Bend, I never doubted that the Outreach and Rural Studios' work would leave the community far better off than it had been previously. What were literally shacks have been replaced with adequate housing enhanced by striking architectural character. Functional alternatives have replaced waste water systems ill suited to the local soil conditions. Education and better access to human services have improved public health. A community chapel, which now occupies what was once the site of a discarded school bus, provides a new sense of collective identity for a place that previously had none.

Completing the school bus shelter that is centrally located for use by most of the children in Mason's Bend.

It is impossible to deny that these changes have benefited Mason's Bend, but in a world where the only constant is change, what will happen when outreach efforts move on to other communities? Would conditions return to their prior sad state, or would our efforts generate a perpetual energy within the community that would invigorate its residents to continue on the path toward a better life? I did not expect to discover the answer in ten weeks, nor do I currently know it. I did, however, realize things that helped me move closer to an answer.

During the summer, witnessing stolen materials, minor vandalism, and residents' general lack of concern for issues outside the personal sphere of Mason's Bend eroded a lot of confidence in someone who had volunteered to work in 100-degree temperatures. There were many instances when the most pessimistic opinions of outreach recipients seemed to hold some real weight. But I also had to optimistically believe that, while there is no all-encompassing means of relief to poverty, there is a solution, for each individual community. In a scene from Stanley Kubrick's *Full Metal Jacket*, a reporter asks an infantry Marine if the United States belongs in Vietnam. After a moment of thought, he replies, "I don't know, but I think I belong here." Half the solution, I realized, is being willing to continually immerse yourself in the situation until you can come up with a thoughtful response.

If I had to describe what I did in Alabama that I thought would have the biggest impact, I would have to borrow a term from the nonviolence movement of the Civil Rights era: "direct civil action." This is what Dr. Martin Luther King, Jr., believed was the best method of accomplishing the things that he saw needed to be done. The idea of getting actively involved in the search for a solution is one of the lasting impressions I carried away from my experiences in Alabama that summer. Looking back, I do not know if we had the right answer, but I believe we moved toward the right solution by trying.

THE FUTURE OF OUTREACH PROGRAMS

I think outreach efforts should continue in our society, if for no other reason, because they can. Beyond the fact that we live in the richest and most powerful nation in the world, within every person there lies some responsibility to improve, whether it be himself or the surrounding environment. I saw many things that summer that attacked my beliefs in social programs, but I also saw many things that buoyed my belief in opportunity. I heard a man who probably has no more than a few years of formal education speak like a Nobel laureate

Mason's Bend children make use of the summer's work.

when he told his wife, who was too ill to attend the dedication of the community chapel, that their marriage had made them one. It was incredible to hear him explain that one of them being there was the same as both. I am aware of the dangers of aestheticizing poverty, but for all the problems I saw affecting the Black Belt in Alabama, I cannot help but remember the simplicity of life as extraordinarily enlightening. I refuse to believe that there can be no hope for change in a place that obviously has so much potential.

One of Isaac Newton's laws of motion states that for every action there is an equal and opposite reaction. During ten weeks with the Outreach Studio, I found that my experience had as much of an effect on me as I hoped it would on the community in which I worked. My own expectations waxed and waned as the summer progressed, but by our tenure's end, we had produced a healthy body of work that included a community recreation pavilion for Mason's Bend, as well as corresponding benefits within ourselves for having attempted the endeavor.

Despite the progress we made, I still find myself with questions and concerns about the success of our efforts. I am convinced that continued outreach efforts are the first step to success, but, impatient, I realize that I will have to let time reveal the final answers. In the meantime, I will continue to search for new opportunities to do those things that still need to get done.

FURTHER FORWARD: OPERATIVE PRACTICES

JASON PEARSON

JASON PEARSON is the author of *University-Community Design Partnerships: Innovations in Practice* and the director of strategy at Greenblue, a design-based nonprofit organization. His recent research on alternative strategies for practice focuses on identifying opportunities that support innovations in sustainable design practice.

The projects and ideas documented in this volume are inspiring examples of a vitally important, but frequently overlooked, area of architecture: innovations in practice. The impact that they achieve goes far beyond merely including underserved populations in the roster of clients benefiting from architectural services. They also engage a wide range of activities that significantly broaden and deepen the possibilities of contemporary practice. These activities range from community organizing to political advocacy, from volunteer fund-raising to strategic leadership.

This expansion of the scope of architectural practice is based on participants' shared recognition of the inadequacy of conventional design strategies and practice models to address the full complexity of contemporary social, political, and environmental challenges, particularly among economically challenged communities. Conventional design practice models are insufficient instruments for achieving meaningful social, economic, and political change in many complex contexts. At the same time the design process can be a valuable platform from which to deploy other strategies that are effective, either independently or in conjunction with traditional design strategies.

The projects documented here are innovative not only in their materiality or program, but also in their modes of practice and production. They offer a rare look at contemporary advances in architectural practice, advances that are relevant not only to the specific challenges of community-based design, but also to the broader practice of architecture.

This points the way to a standard of comprehensive excellence in architecture, a more demanding measure by which to evaluate the achievements of designers and their work. For these projects go beyond the physical innovations in form, material, and technology, or even the programmatic innovations in representation and function, that are the dominant subjects of contemporary architectural discourse. Without in any way sacrificing excellence in these areas, they achieve, at the same time, a multidimensional, strategic excellence in practice that raises the bar for all architects.

Programs like Archeworks, Atlanta CHRC, City Design Center, Design Corps, Hamer Center, Nirmithi Kendras, Outreach Studio, Pratt PICCED, Project Row Houses, Rice Building Workshop, Rural Studio, Small Town Design Center, and the many others documented here act as agents of change by mobilizing innovative strategies not bound by traditional definitions of design. The architects and designers who lead these efforts do not worry about whether or not what they do is architecture, whether or not their strategies are design strategies, or whether the product of their work is embodied in built form, but pursue whatever combination of means are available to achieve change in a given context. Their work is more than just an assembly of alternative practices. Instead, it contributes to the increasing diversity of strategies available to all architects.

DEFINING OPERATIVE PRACTICES

As a tentative contribution to the appreciation of such strategic innovations in architectural practice—an effort pioneered by Robert Gutman in *Architectural Practice: A Critical View* and furthered by Dana Cuff in *Architecture: The Story of Practice* and Diane Ghirardo in *Out of Site*, I offer here a new term, "operative practices," to link parallel architectural strategies of formal, programmatic, and tactical innovation. Simply put, operative practices are intentional, creative actions—formal, programmatic, fiscal, functional, physical, social, political, aesthetic, or otherwise—that achieve positive, lasting change. The definition is deliberately broad, and could be usefully applied to work of any profession or discipline that aims to transform the world in positive ways. But it has particular relevance for the work of designers, whose operative practices can be discovered in the moments where the process and/or products of design engage existing contexts so as to transform them in concerted, critical, and positive ways. Echoing this book's title, operative design practices produce results that not only look good, but do good, too.

My purpose here is to nudge critical language about architecture toward something that includes, in the spirit of this publication, the diversity of approaches demanded by the increasingly complex challenges of contemporary design. By opening the profession to these complexities, operative practices realize architecture's latent potential to vitally engage a community's social organization and cultural identity. In so doing, such practices—and the critical language that describes them—enable us to assess, compare, and value innovative achievements across conventional categories of physical form, social use, and professional practice.

By reframing the value of design, architects can expand the definition of creativity and innovation from the physical products of design to include the dynamic relationships that are created between those products and their systemic contexts. A new understanding of design practice as a vehicle for operative practice focuses attention on the ways in which a design of any scale—from consumer product to urban plan—affects in substantial ways the physical, cultural, historical, political, and economic systems in which it is engaged. Operative practice suggests a model of design that engages the boundaries between objects, agents, and contexts, insisting that the ambitions of a designer lie in the creative restructuring and reformulation of these boundaries themselves.

OPERATIVE PRACTICES AT WORK

Successful operative practices are vital in achieving broad social objectives. They are approaches that individual, government, nonprofit, and for-profit agents alike should deploy frequently and strategically. It is in this light that I would characterize the great significance of the projects and ideas documented in this book.

In the work of Roberta Feldman at the City Design Center in Chicago, for instance, the practice of design, driven by a strong mission of social justice, explicitly aims to restructure relationships between those who make community design decisions and those who are affected by them. The context on which the practice operates is the political process itself, and Feldman evaluates its success and failure by the degree to which it is able to effectively transform this context in meaningful ways. The successful brokering of an accord between competing CDCs during the development of the Chicago Imagebase project, for instance, represents a powerful demonstration of the transformative impact of the work of the City Design Center on its local context, and therefore a fine example of excellence in operative practice. Similarly, when Feldman's ambitions are suppressed in the development report for a small Illinois town, she is frustrated at the failure to make an impact on the political process in the town, the failure to operate effectively on her chosen context, the failure to achieve excellence in operative practice.

Other examples from this book document attempts to simultaneously transform multiple aspects of the contexts on which practitioners work. At Bayview, Maurice Cox, RBGC, The Nature Conservancy, the EPA, and their partners from within and outside the Bayview community endeavored to achieve lasting, systemic change in the multiple physical, cultural, political, and economic systems that affect the village and its residents by deploying a range of traditional and nontraditional design and nondesign strategies. The existing conditions upon which they sought to operate included physical challenges (lack of running water, unsanitary toilet facilities, leaking buildings, poor storm-water management), political challenges (lack of political leverage), and socioeconomic challenges (poverty), and their approach was appropriately multidimensional and complex. In fact, of the array of strategies described by Cox, very few were oriented toward the development of a physical plan for the village, but all contributed in targeted ways to the remediation of systemic challenges facing the village. I suggest these strategies as examples of operative practices by virtue of this plural, systematic approach.

Elsewhere, innovations through operative practice are most evident in transformations of traditional modes of design service. In the work of Archeworks, Design Corps, Rural Studio, Studio 804, and other education-based design initiatives, the systemic context upon which the practices operate is often the anonymous, standardized processes of government low-income housing and service provision, and notably the failure of these processes to accommodate many individuals' and families' specific needs. In response, each of these organizations has developed a unique, replicable model of design service provision by strategically coupling government and nonprofit funding with the talents of student designers or design interns in a streamlined, low-cost design process: a new model of practice in response to a unique political and economic context. Though the process of design service provided in each case is perfectly consistent with traditional approaches to private design practice, their innovations as operative practice lie in their singular methods of funding and delivery, not to mention their transformation of the traditional model of architectural education and internship. An even more stringent measure of their success may be their ability to transform the larger systemic context of funding and delivery on which they operate, for instance through incorporation of the "Direct-to-You" strategies developed by Design Corps into the same federal systems of low-cost housing provision to which they currently present a minority alternative.

Finally, the work of Scott Ball at CHRC in Atlanta exhibits two examples of emergent operative practices. First, in Ball's work as Director of Emergency Repair at CHRC, his "ishy" approach to nudging and tweaking emergency repair projects represents a strategic operation on traditional expectations for design excellence. In other contexts, settling for a house that was sturdyish, flattish, or straightish might be seen as a failure in construction standards or political will. But Ball's insistence on these "ishy" solutions as successes in the context of affordable housing in the city of Atlanta, by altering the standards of success themselves, actively alters the conditions in which he works, and thereby creates more quality affordable housing for less capital cost. Ball's new partnerships with building product manufacturers are another example of operative practices. By carving out a niche for CHRC in the design of showcase projects that include new building products in an affordable housing context, Ball not only enhances the willingness of affordable housing providers and consumers to consider new and innovative design solutions, but also builds interest in the product manufacturer community in the development of new products for affordable housing markets, operating simultaneously on the expectations of housing providers and product manufacturers. In both cases, Ball's ability to create alternative definitions of quality and innovation in response to local particularities leads to a transformation of the very context in which he works, thereby meeting his claim that by "applying our skills to society's needs in new ways, we will reinvent architecture."

It should be clear, from these diverse examples, that operative practices will always be locally specific and necessitate a constant reinvention of the criteria by which we judge design excellence. Where some might see substantial, positive change in existing contexts and systems, others might see a negative persistence of the status quo. But such potential difficulties in applying this terminology are the very basis of its value. Individual disagreements will arise over whether a particular project or strategy can achieve lasting, positive, cultural, physical, economic, or political change in its context, but the value of operative practice lies in its insistence that the ambition for such change is a worthwhile and legitimate ambition for design practice, and that our assessment of design excellence must include this debate.

If use of the term opens up the field of possible action, allowing us to argue not about whether we are entitled to say, "I am an architect," but about whether we are entitled to say, "I am an agent of positive change," not about whether we meet status quo standards of design excellence, but whether we achieve change that is meaningful by standards appropriate to a given context, then it may provide us a framework on which to predicate action, and it may represent a true structure for inclusion in the spirit of this publication.

CREDITS

Project credits:

FINDING CLIENTS, BRYAN BELL
Rural Studio Family Selection Process:
Students: Rebecca Alvord, Jason Andoscia,
Felicia Atwell, Matt Barrett, Jennifer Bonner,
Jonathan Graves, Emily King, Robert Littleton,
Mary Beth Maness, John McCabe, Marion
McElroy, Nathan Orrison, Jennifer Saville,
Jeff Slaton, David Snyder, Daniel Sweeney,
Emmie Wayland
Instructors: Bryan Bell, Stephen Hoffman

DIRECT-TO-YOU, KRISTINE J. RENNER WADE
Direct-to-You Design Program: Bryan Bell,
Ethan Cohen, Ryan Giblin, Kristine Wade,
Enrique Zuniga

TIMELY TACTICS, MICHAEL RIOS
Collaborators: FROSI Partners, The Unity Council,
The Trust for Public Land, City of Oakland Parks
Department, University/Oakland Metropolitan
Forum
Union Point Park Design Team I (conceptual
design and master plan): Scott Donahue, Randy
Hester, Jeff Hou, Ned Kahn, Gabriel Miel, Michael
Rios, San Francisco office of EDAW, Inc., U.C.
Berkeley Department of Landscape Architecture
and Environmental Planning students
Union Point Park Design Team II (design develop-
ment and construction drawings): Patillo &
Garrett Associates, Mario Schjetnan Garduno of
Grupo de Diseno Urbano

MAKING A STUDIO PROJECT REAL,
VICTORIA BALLARD BELL
Design: Victoria Ballard Bell; assistance from
Seth Peterson
Funding: National Endowment for the Arts, U.S.
Department of Housing and Urban Development

USE OF DESIGN WITH HABITAT FOR
HUMANITY, EVAN HARREL
Habitat House Design: Paul Homeyer, Gensler

REBUILDING BAYVIEW, MAURICE D. COX
Master Planning and Phase 1 Design:
Maurice Cox, lead designer and facilitator, with
RBGC Architecture.Research.Urbanism, Partners:
Craig Barton, Giovanna Galfione, Marthe Rowen
UVA Student Assistants: Susannah Mills,
Patrick Slater
RBGC Collaborators: Tim Ciccone, Celia Liu,
Esther Yang
Design Corps Interns: Jeff Evans, Will Hartzog

Environmental Planning: Vladimir Gavrilovic,
Paradigm Design; William A. Drevry, Old Dominion
University; Sarah Amthor, Paul Bull, ODU Student
Assistants; Steve Parker, The Nature Conservancy

SORE SHOULDERS, BRUISED ETHICS,
SCOTT WING
House of Modest Means Instructors: Scott Wing,
Eva Kultermann
Students: David Belviy, Thaddeus Bryniarski, Jon
Cordi, Sam Friday, Matt Galbraith, Chase Garrett,
Casey Hargrove, Kenton Keeter, Ryan King,
Jessica Lewallen, Kelly Moloney, Bobby Nixon,
Shannon Passmore, Kenny Roberts, Mike Spaeth,
Andrea Sturgis, David Tanner, Aaron Wenger,
Randy Wolf

ACTIVIST PRACTICE, ROBERTA M. FELDMAN
Brown School Play Lot Design: Philip Enquist
and Toni Griffin, Skidmore Owings and Merrill in
association with the University of Illinois at
Chicago City Design Center

DREAMTREE PROJECT, MARK S. GOLDMAN
Architectural Design: Mark S. Goldman
Architect of Record: Craig Lyman, AIA
Contractor of Record: Onyx Construction/Design
HVAC Consultant: Jim Thompson
Teen Construction Crew: Rocky Mountain
Youth Corps
RMYC Supervisor: Scott Evans
Onyx Construction Foreman: Tim Gaskins
Onyx Construction Crew: Gerald Bernal, Jose
Casares, Heru Hardijanto, Chris Hummel, Frank
Macias, Ian McNairy, Ben Ortgea, Ian Goldman
Sanderson, Todd Thompson, Thomas Valdez,
Omar Villareal
Mechanical Contractors: Tom Bishop's Plumbing
& Dobry Water Systems
Electrical Contractor: Nick Stollard, PDC Electric
Plaster Contractor: Plastering Plus
Concrete Countertops: Frank Clements
Painted Floors: Susan Kohl
Tile Mosaics: Chris Taylor
Stone Carving: Mark Saxe, South West Stone
Decorative Painting: Cami Hartman, Kim Treiber
Log Ceiling Design / Round Room: John Szerdi, AIA
Concrete Flatwork: LCI 2 Contractors
Adobe Press: Dharma Properties

MOBILE STUDIO, MARALEE GABLER
Johnsonburg Mobile Studio Team: Richard
Allen, Bryan Bell, Sam Dennis, Bill Elmendorf,

Jeff Evans, Kelleann Foster, MaraLee Gabler, Mark Hood, Loukas Kalisperis, Neil Korostoff, Andy Lefkowitz, Christina Marts, Michael Rios, Bill Shuffstall, Scott Wing

EXPANDING THE ROLE OF THE ARCHITECT, M. SCOTT BALL
Moseley Residence Design: Scott Ball, Community Housing Resource Center
Client: Shawn Moseley

COMMUNICATION, ANDREA DIETZ
Community Bulletin Board: Designer: Andrea Dietz; Design-Build Team: Bryan Bell, Andrea Dietz, Jeff Evans, Kersten Harries, Seth Peterson, Lesli Stinger
TUCCA Barbecue Pavilion: Designer: Lesli Stinger; Design-Build Team: Bryan Bell, Andrea Dietz, Jeff Evans, Kersten Harries, Seth Peterson, Lesli Stinger
TUCCA Community Center: Designer: Andrea Dietz; Renderings: Jason Dufilho

THE ROLE OF THE CITIZEN ARCHITECT, SAMUEL MOCKBEE
Design-Build Team: Floris Keverling Buisman, Ben Cannard, Philip Crosscup, Kerry Larkin, Marie Richard, James Michael Tate, Keith Zawistowski
Supervising Instructors: Samuel Mockbee, Andrew Freear, Jay Sanders

ARCHITECTURE AS ARTIFACT, BRYAN BELL
Migrant Housing Design Team: Bryan Bell, Kersten Harries, Melissa Tello Poole, Vicente Sauceda, Lesli Stinger, Krisztina Tokes, Kindra Welch

LIGHT, JAE CHA
Church in Urubo, Bolivia:
Architect: Jae Cha
Collaborator: Zack Hemmelgarn (3-D rendering)
Construction: People of Urubo, Alex & Co., KCPC Bolivia STM 2000
Sponsors: Kie Dong Lee, Deuk Soo Jung

SIX-SQUARE HOUSE, KIM NEUSCHELER
Design: Kim Neuscheler, Katherine Dy
Instructors: Danny Samuels, Nonya Grenader
Contributor: Rick Lowe, Project Row Houses

ARCHEWORKS, MONICA CHADHA
Team Members: Jitendre Barlinge (architecture/software design), Laura Fallace

(graphic and set design), Ann Melichar (interior design, law), Nelson White (urban preservation, architecture theory), Judy Jacobson (system analysis), Frances Whitehead (artist and teacher, School of Art Institute of Chicago)
Funding: National Endowment for the Arts Design Access Program
Thanks to focus group participants, the staff at Access Living, Bill Armstrong at the Rehabilitation Institute of Chicago, Eric Huffman, and the residents of Over the Rainbow for their support, input, and encouragement throughout the project.

SMALL TOWN CENTER, SHANNON CRISS
Third Year Design Studio:
Instructors: Nils Gore, Shannon Criss
Student team: Tim Anson, Benji Armstrong, Noel Bendure, John Bondurant, Joey Brown, Matt Buchanan, Laura Butler, Kiley Chase, Tommy Chisholm, Pam Clark, Todd Clark, Lisa Cuevas, Bree Dodson, Tim Duboise, Jesse Farley, Garrett Goodman, Wes Harp, Danellen Johnson, Kelly Kavitz, Julie Kern, Kyle Kish, Barry Lann, Tim Lin, Ryan McQuade, Paul Mitchell, Chris Myers, Casey Newman, Noelle Norman, Thomas Price, Randy Sappington, Laura Smith, Newell Watkins
Funding: CREATE Foundation, the Mississippi Arts Foundation, Chickasaw County, the City of Okolona

KU STUDIO 804, JESSICA BRISTOW
Members of Studio 804, 2001: Chad Bristow, Jessica Bristow, Brenda Brosa, Jaimi Fisher, René Goethel, Joe Keal, Mark LaMair, Scott McMurray, Michael Miller, Lou Nunez, Alexis Phillips, Nathan Rapp, Suzanne Regier, Mike Rosso, Ryan Warman, Billy Williams

OUTREACH STUDIO, MARCUS HURLEY
Instructors: Samuel Mockbee, Bryan Bell, Stephen Hoffman
Outreach Studio Fellows: Marcus Hurley, Scott Marek, Rasheda McCalpine, David Ranghelli, Claudia Richardson, Samantha Rinehart, Heath Lee VanFleet

Image credits:

1 / TOOLS FOR CHANGE
23–26: Bryan Bell; 27: (top left) Jennifer
Bonner, (top right, bottom) Bryan Bell; 28–29:
Kersten Harries; 31–32, 36: Through the Lens;
35: Ryan Chin and Louie Tak Wing, from Sara Har,
"Home Work," in *Architecture* 88:9 (September
1999): 134; 37–39, 43: Bryan Bell; 41–42: Brian
King; 45–46, 49 (bottom): Pattillo & Garrett
Associates and Mario Schjetnan Garduno of
Grupo de Diseno Urbano; 49: (top left) Michael
Rios, (top right) Jeff Hou; 50: Trust for Public
Land; 53–58: Victoria Ballard Bell.

2 / TUNING ESTABLISHED MODELS
61–64, 68: PICCED; 66: Public domain; 71–75:
Paul Homeyer; 77–83: Scott Wing; 85–91: Amy
Hause; 93–96: Red Feather Development Group;
97: Janey Terry.

3 / BUILDING WITH A COMMUNITY
101–102: Giovanna Galfione; 103: (top) Susannah
Mills, (bottom) Curtis Badger; 104–108: RBGC
Architecture.Research.Urbanism; 109–113:
courtesy Roberta M. Feldman; 115–123: Photo-
works; 125–131: Hamer Center for Community
Design Assistance; 133–140: CHRC; 141–142,
147: Jason Dufilho; 143, 145 (bottom), 148:
Bryan Bell; 145 (top): Lesli Stinger.

4 / RELATING SOCIAL NEEDS TO DESIGN
151–155: Timothy Hursley; 157–158, 161–162:
Fiset Miller Bourke Architects; 160: Jean-Lou
Hamelin; 163: Lynn Jacobs, Kahnawake
Environment Office; 165–173: Patricia Evans;
175–176, 181 (bottom): Matt Heckendorn; 177:
Chris Johnson; 178: Vicente Sauceda, Bryan Bell;
181 (top, center): Bryan Bell; 183–184, 187, 188
(left), 189 (bottom): Daniel Lama; 186: Zack
Hemmelgarn; 188 (right), 189 (top): Jae Cha.

5 / LOOKING DEEPER INTO DESIGN-BUILD
193–194, 196, 199 (right): Rice Building Workshop; 195, 198 (left), 199 (left): Kim Neuscheler;
197: Kim Neuscheler and Kathy Dy; 198 (right):
Nonya Grenader; 203–208: Archeworks;
209–210, 215: Laura Butler; 212, 216: Small
Town Center; 213, 214 (bottom): Nils Gore; 214
(top): Barry Lann; 217–218, 221: Scott McMurray;
219, 223 (left), 224: René Goethel; 222: Jessica
Bristow; 223 (right): Dan Rockhill; 225–226, 230:
Tim Hursley; 227–229: Bryan Bell.